Ex Libris

Lesley Campbell.

Psychology and Medicine

S. J. Rachman and Clare Philips

PSYCHOLOGY
and
MEDICINE

Temple Smith · London

First published in Great Britain in 1975
by Maurice Temple Smith Ltd
37 Great Russell Street, LONDON WC1

© 1975 S. J. Rachman and Clare Philips

ISBN 0 8511 7066 8

Printed in Great Britain by
Clarke, Doble & Brendon Ltd
Plymouth

Contents

	Foreword by Professor H. J. Eysenck	7
1	Psychology in medicine	13
2	Doctor's orders	22
3	Pain	43
4	A psychological approach to headaches	56
5	Sleep disorders	70
6	Placebo power	89
7	Self-control of bodily functions	103
8	Reducing health risks by self-control	123
9	Psychiatric psychology	138
10	The psychological impact of admission to hospital	165
11	Custodians or teachers?	178
12	Projects and prospects	193
	Notes	205
	Acknowledgements	215
	Index	217

To Bob and Monica

Foreword

Medicine has undergone many changes in its long history; at present it is changing rapidly in two opposite directions. On the one hand, it is becoming markedly more impersonal; this is due to two trends which are difficult to halt or reverse. The great revolution inaugurated when the National Health Service was first planned has led to more and more use being made of the state-provided facilities, until now each patient is seen for such a short time that personal contact between doctor and patient lasts on the average only five minutes—and may be much shorter than that! Many doctors complain that this reduces them to the status of government clerks, and makes it impossible for them to practise medicine as they were taught to as students. At the same time, the massive increase in medical knowledge and expertise has made it impossible for anyone to know in detail more than a small area; consequently, the treatment of all but the most obvious disorders has been transferred from the general practitioner to the hospital consultant. But the patient who goes into hospital immediately becomes an impersonal object, a mere statistic or case in an everlasting parade before the consultant and his students, valued more for the interest of his condition than for his intrinsic human importance. Medical men have protested against this bureaucratic aspect of medicine, but it is difficult to see how the trend can be reversed; the social forces which have produced these changes are still active.

7

Patients, too, have often protested against impersonal treatment, but equally without success. Clearly, there is a problem here which society disregards at its peril.

On the other hand, the medical world is becoming more and more convinced that the consideration of the patient as an individual is at least as important as other factors in the treatment of his disease; our increasing knowledge of psychosomatic disorders has added impetus to the demand that we should treat the patient, not the disease. This demand clearly goes counter to the trends listed in the first paragraph; while it is being ever more clearly recognised that we should look at the patient as a person, the social trend is in the opposite direction. Medicine for the few can recognise the importance of the personal element; could a state medical service do the same? The main argument of this important new book seems to be that this is possible, but only if we agree to yet another great change in medical treatment. This change implies that psychological factors are important in therapy, and that the psychologist should be an equal member in the medical team. The argument is based on facts which medical men cannot disregard, and which demonstrate clearly that non-medical factors cooperate closely with medical ones in determining the success of treatment.

Let us look at just one example. Most doctors would probably agree that research into the improvement of certain drug treatments would be much more important than research into social compliance, as carried out by psychologists. Yet let us look at the facts. As Dr Rachman and Dr Philips show, only a minority of patients take the drugs prescribed for them by their doctors at the right time and in the right quantity. From the point of view of medical effectiveness, it would be much more useful to get patients to comply with the doctor's instructions and take their drugs properly than to improve marginally the usefulness of drugs which patients do not take anyway. If one of the reasons for the failure of patients to comply with the doctors' dispensation is the latters' failure to treat them as individuals, and if psychologists can demonstrate how this difficulty can be overcome, then clearly they have shown their right to be admitted as part of the general medical team, with an important, if circumscribed, role, the importance of which is likely to grow as the sociological trends just discussed work themselves out more and more.

This is not the only way in which medicine and psychology interact; the authors make many important suggestions, and quote many relevant facts, to demonstrate the reality of this interaction. Medicine, as well as popular imagination, have usually followed Descartes's view of the complete separation of body and mind; this dualism puts medicine and psychology on different sides of the watershed, and leaves little possibility of any coming together. But experimental work carried out during the last half-century, both in physiology and psychology, leaves little doubt that this dualistic notion is in fact erroneous, and that we would be much better advised to follow Spinoza and his doctrine of the 'double aspect' of the body–mind phenomena—identical causes, viewed from opposite sides. Pain, to take but one of the examples discussed in detail in this book, is not simply a physiological effect; there are physical and psychological elements involved in the perception of pain, and it would be idle to deny the importance of either. The total effect—the perceived pain—can be studied and viewed from either side, and should certainly be experimented upon with both positions in mind; but we cannot hope to gain a complete understanding of the phenomenon unless we look at it from this 'double aspect'. Medical treatment has traditionally looked only at the physical side, and has made many important advances along these lines; the time has come to admit that there are inherent limitations to this tradition, and that great advances are possible by taking into account the psychological factor as well. This is an addition, not a substitute; the two aspects are equally real and equally important—there is no intention to substitute an empty idealism for an over-simplified realism.

With great skill, and much learning, Dr Rachman and Dr Philips spell out some of the ways in which such a programme could be implemented, using little-known research results to buttress their arguments. They are emphatic on one point: psychology has hitherto been associated almost exclusively with psychiatry, and most medical people regard this liaison as almost God-given, in the mistaken belief that both psychology and psychiatry deal with the 'mind'. This is not true of psychiatry, and it is not true of psychology; both deal with behaviour. And, as the authors emphasise, so does medicine; making prescriptions, and telling patients how to take their pills, are aspects of behaviour (on the part of the doctor), while failure to understand the prescription, and neglect in taking the pills, are aspects of behaviour also (on the part of the patient, this time). The psychologist has an important part to play in analysing these different forms of behaviour, and in suggesting ways in which they could be improved. He is not concerned with the content of the prescription, but he is concerned with the manner in which it is made; the failure of medicine to realise the importance of this latter aspect has led to much unhappiness and lack of success for otherwise well-planned treatments.

Perhaps the statement that psychology is not concerned with the content of the prescription is not quite accurate. If a pill is prescribed to a patient who complains of difficulties in going to sleep, or to another patient who is anxious and depressed, then the psychologist would not presume to doubt the doctor's right to choose which pill to prescribe. But he might draw attention to the fact that sleeplessness and anxiety are behavioural problems as much as medical ones, and that there are behavioural methods of treatment which might be superior to medical ones—in the sense of having fewer side-effects, of curing the underlying problem rather than side-stepping it, and of being more appropriate for the complaint in question. Many problems which are at the moment classed as 'medical' are in fact largely behavioural, demanding re-education rather than treatment, and for these psychologists have worked out ways of modifying behaviour which are quite independent of medicine as ordinarily understood. In many other cases the patient's complaint lies on the borderline between medicine and psychology, requiring cooperation between doctor and psychologist. In yet other cases, the underlying problem is clearly medical, but associated with it are psychological problems which must be solved in order to give the medical treatment the best chance of success. Many examples of all these different types of problems are given in the course of the book; it is to be hoped that medical practitioners reading it will see the advantage to themselves of handing over intractable problems which their education does not fit them to deal with to experts who are willing to have a go—and who have shown in the past that they do have methods which can with advantage be used in these cases to reach the required end.

From the point of view of the medical man, there are great advantages in delegating these problems to the psychologist, and in concentrating on those problems which his training fits him for. In following the path laid out here by the two authors the community would greatly benefit. At the moment a great deal of money goes into a National Health Service, in which much that is done by highly paid doctors could in fact be done better by less highly paid psychologists, leaving doctors to do their proper job. Research in applied psychology might give dividends even richer than research in medicine directly. There are many advantages for psychology, too, in such a scheme. Psychologists can in this way test their theories in practice, and they can gain access to new facts which may serve to strengthen and improve their theories.

It is often a disadvantage to be startlingly original—the *Zeitgeist*, that elusive spirit of the times which seems always to lag behind the truly seminal developments of any age, sees to it that the prophet is scorned for pointing out the path to the future. This book may escape this fate by appearing at a time when the disadvantages of the present lines of development are becoming clear to most people—doctors and patients alike. This does not mean that its recommendations will be accepted without argument, nor would the authors themselves want such an easy victory. They are hoping to start a discussion of their proposals, in the confident expectation that those best fitted to contribute to this discussion will decide how psychologists can best play their part in the Health Service. They have provided the arguments and the evidence; it is now up to society to evaluate their proposals, and to act on this evaluation. Doctors and patients may both have reason to be grateful to the authors for their labours.

H. J. EYSENCK

Institute of Psychiatry, University of London

12

1 Psychology in medicine

Within the medical profession there is a growing appreciation of the importance of psychological factors in what is sometimes called the 'process of becoming ill'. It is also agreed that psychological factors contribute to the process of recovery. Unfortunately psychologists have been slow to recognise and respond to the need for a psychological approach to problems of illness and health, outside psychiatry. The main purpose of this book is to present a case for widening the scope of clinical psychology to include medical problems as well as those of a psychiatric character. We feel that the expansion is feasible as well as desirable and illustrate our general theme with examples from the psychology of pain, sleep disturbances, placebos and pill-taking, among others.

The great advances in medical knowledge registered over the last fifty years have not led to the declining need for medical services predicted by social reformers. Illnesses such as tuberculosis, diphtheria and pneumonia, which formerly resulted in premature deaths, are controlled, and many serious and handicapping illnesses of former years are now managed well enough to allow people to live a full life. Over the same period, however, we have seen a greater number of referrals and admissions to hospitals, a growing demand for medical investigations and even larger increases in prescriptions and rates of absence because of sickness. The paradox is neatly expressed in a publication of the Office of

13

Health Economics (OHE), *Medicine and Society*: 'While the population in absolute terms has clearly become healthier, it is nevertheless seeking and receiving very much more medical treatment.'[1] The control of the most serious illnesses has been followed by an increase in requests for medical assistance in coping with lesser problems, discomforts and minor illnesses.

[The public] perceive and act on symptoms which previously they would have ignored. Discomforts which they would have considered irrelevant in the days when premature death and crippling disability from serious disease were commonplace are now thought to justify medical treatment.

As a result, far more attention is being paid to the psychological and social elements in medical services. 'It is realised that much more understanding is needed of the non-medical factors affecting demands for treatment.' The Office of Health Economics publication points out that the 'naïve assumption' that a state of illness is easily defined or easily recognised is 'no longer valid'. It seems that most people feel unwell very frequently (in one London survey, 95 per cent of the respondents had experienced some symptoms during the previous two weeks) and we also know that only a small minority of people consult a doctor when they experience minor symptoms. For the most part, people take self-prescribed remedies on these occasions. A small number of cases are also identifiable in which, despite the presence of serious illness, the potential patient does not recognise or perhaps admit the presence of illness. Others consult their doctors for the most trivial reasons. The point here is that the first definition of the presence of illness is made by the person affected, usually in conjunction with close relatives. It is not, in

the first instance, a medical decision. Recent information has also shown that tolerance for minor discomforts
and distress varies in members of different groups. In
one industrial study, it was possible to distinguish
between employees who were frequently sick and those
who were rarely sick. People who were dissatisfied with
their jobs, or had family troubles, or unstable personalities, were absent through sickness three times more often
than a comparison group of stable people. In another
context entirely, it was found that the main determinant
of whether a child was sent to a guidance clinic for
medical consultation was to be found in the mother's
attitude to the child and his problem.[2] The OHE report
points out that 'an increasing proportion of the workload in general practice concerns social and psychological problems rather than physical ones'. The report
goes on, 'The needs which people are expressing when
they consult their doctor as a reaction to their social
(or psychological) situation are very real, even if they
are not medical in the traditional sense'. It is argued
that if the medical profession is to accept these requests
for assistance as legitimate demands on their time and
service, medical education will 'need to be even further
broadened' into the related disciplines of psychology
and sociology. 'The medical schools must in the future
also concentrate more on teaching general practitioners
about human behaviour, rather than merely extending
their technical medical knowledge.'

Steps towards a medical psychology

Psychologists failed to respond to these important
psychological changes in general medical care because
of their almost exclusive concern with psychiatric problems. Bearing in mind the fact that psychology is the

study of behaviour and experience, there is no longer any reason why applied psychology should be restricted to psychiatric abnormalities, nor is there any satisfactory reason for clinical psychologists to ignore or avoid the vast number of behavioural problems which arise in all aspects of health services. In this book, we introduce and consider some new possibilities which an enlargement of the scope of clinical psychology would offer. We have not attempted to produce a detailed or systematic exposition of these possibilities but, rather, to introduce ideas. In some of the chapters we give a methodical account of one subject, such as pain, while in other chapters we provide a bird's-eye view of the subject supplemented by concrete proposals and recommendations.

At present the title 'medical psychology' is taken to mean something close to psychiatric psychology. There is no reason for retaining this exceedingly narrow definition; 'medical psychology' should refer to *all* the applications of normal and abnormal psychology to medicine.

We are advocating no less than a fundamental change in the scope of clinical psychology. Many psychologists have started on the work of reappraising their discipline, some belatedly[3] and others presciently,[4, 5, 6] but almost all of them with optimism. Most psychologists will welcome the expansion and, if successful, it would mean that in future they will have to deal with fresh intellectual problems and develop new skills.

It is legitimate to ask, however, what the medical profession can expect to gain. In the first place, they would receive additional assistance in dealing with certain types of clinical problem. In the longer run, the theory of medicine might be enriched and the practice of medicine regain some lost interest and personal

16

rewards. The infusion of psychology might also help to smooth the inevitable transition from paternalistic medicine to newer forms. It could help doctors to establish more satisfactory personal relationships with their patients and to develop their important educational functions. Patients, in turn, would be encouraged to become less dependent on their doctors and to play an active part in maintaining their own health.

One cannot argue with history. To a large extent clinical psychology grew up in the shadow of psychiatry. There is little doubt that this relationship was mutually beneficial, despite the unnecessary limitations that were placed on psychologists. Having acquired considerable knowledge about abnormal behaviour and expertise in its assessment and modification, it would be foolish to abandon the application of psychology to psychiatric problems (see Chapter 9).

Some of the applications of psychology which we will discuss have already been the subject of clinical work and research while others are speculative. We discuss the potential and actual psychological contributions to problems of pain, sleep disorders, pill-taking, intellectual retardation, hospital admissions, doctor–patient relationships, failure to comply with medical advice, smoking, obesity, headaches, cardiac disorders, psychiatric disturbances and some psychosomatic disorders. There are many other common problems that are not taken up here at any length; among them are child development, sexual disorders and speech disorders.

Child psychology is one of the best-developed branches of the subject but it has so far made little impact on medical care, despite the fact that infant and child welfare services are such a valuable part of modern health services. Advice on child care is provided on a large scale, usually by nursing staff. While much

17

of it, born of many years of experience, appears to be useful and sensible, there is no doubt that child psychologists already are in a position to extend and improve the services. This contribution could be made quickly and usefully. If the opportunity is taken, it should be possible in a few years' time to place the advice given to parents on a more scientific basis; to write a psychologist's version of Spock. The work of Patterson is a first step in this direction.[7, 8] Although Spock's reassuring tone is as invaluable as his paediatric advice, his ventures into child psychology are remarkably uncritical.

A subject of immediate medical and nursing concern is the psychological effect of admission to hospital, and other occasions of separation of a child from his parents. The growth of knowledge about normal child development has already helped to clarify a number of the common problems of childhood, including eating and elimination difficulties.[9] Advances in operant conditioning, a type of reward training, are giving rise to a new technology which is already being introduced into clinical child psychology.[7]

As we shall see, a useful start has also been made in attempting to understand the psychological consequences of various types of medical procedures. The recent advances in psycholinguistics, the study of language development and functions, are likely in the future to be relevant in the management of speech disorders, and advances in behavioural genetics are of wider significance.

The effects of active and inert drugs have been investigated extensively within a psychiatric setting by psychologists, and for this reason it is not so much a new departure as an extension into other branches of medicine. The subject of pain is another with which psychologists are already acquainted. As it is a major source of discomfort and complaint among people requesting assistance from the health services, it is reasonable that psychologists should be asked to put greater effort into understanding the nature of pain and its modification—and not simply within psychiatric samples. A related but more specific problem arises in the practice of surgery, where we have a great deal to learn about how patients can best be prepared for operations and, even more challenging, how they can best be assisted to make a rapid and satisfactory recovery. The problems of dental care, especially in the young, have concerned dentists and educationists for a long time, but have attracted few psychologists. It should be possible to develop improved training techniques to ensure that children learn hygienic habits of care of the teeth and prevention of disease. In addition, some of the fear-reduction techniques already used by psychologists (see Chapter 9) have an important part to play in reducing or eliminating the anxiety and distress often involved in dental treatment.

Group techniques

A second, but lesser, development which we would like to encourage is a shift of emphasis from individual casework to the refinement and implementation of group techniques. This change is needed because of the multiplicity of problems which will require attention and the certainty that we will never have sufficient numbers of qualified psychologists to deal with them as long as the present style of concentrating on individual patients is retained. The impossibility of confining almost all their clinical work to individual patients will become

19

increasingly apparent as the scope of psychology is expanded. It is not suggested that individual case-work should be abandoned, but rather that an exclusive concern with individual work will lead to an unrealistic situation in which psychologists are doing more and more work for fewer and fewer people until they are reduced to working with an infinitesimal proportion of the population. There are two ways in which the size of their clinical contribution can be enlarged. Firstly, techniques of group management can be developed and administered. For example, it should be possible to develop procedures designed to suppress or prevent pain and, once available, these can be taught to several people at the same time. Or to take a psychiatric example, the introduction of a token economy system (a reward training method) on a psychiatric ward enables one to provide assistance for twenty to forty patients within the same treatment programme.

A second, general, way in which the contribution of psychologists can be spread to a larger population is through the execution of problem-solving research, the fruits of which can be handed over to members of ancillary professions to administer. For example, if psychologists were able to develop techniques for improving habits of dental hygiene among children, these findings could be passed on to dentists, school doctors, health visitors, nurses and so on.

If the two main proposals advocated here, enlarging the scope of psychology and placing greater emphasis on group work, are adopted a sequence of changes would result. The theory of clinical psychology would have to be expanded to include the application of psychological science to behavioural problems which arise in psychologically normal people who have general medical problems. This change in orientation would have many practical consequences. First, the training and preparation of psychologists would have to be altered to give them a more general clinical education. It would also follow that although a minority of clinical psychologists would continue to work in psychiatric settings, the majority would be employed in hospitals, community health centres, social service departments and allied agencies. Current clinical practice which concentrates on assessments, based on standardised psychological tests, counselling and modification of abnormal behaviour would have to develop into new shapes. The relative importance of psychometric test assessments would diminish, while counselling and modification techniques would have to be extended beyond the field of abnormal behaviour. Two types of undertaking would become increasingly important: the establishment of new systems of guidance and care within the health services, and the development of trouble-shooting psychologists who might be called into any part of the hospital or health services whenever a behavioural difficulty is proving to be an obstacle to the administration and acceptance of required or desired treatment or prevention plans (for example, failures of diabetic patients to give themselves their insulin injections). The scope of psychological research would have to be expanded and psychologists would need to display some boldness in entering uncharted waters. Perhaps the first and essential step is to change our view of what constitutes a psychological problem. We are convinced that a few months spent wandering around a general hospital or in general practice would produce a profusion of research problems for any psychologist.

2 Doctor's orders

Research has shown that the majority of patients express overall satisfaction with the medical care they receive, in or out of hospital.[1, 2] A significant minority express some dissatisfaction and one of their major complaints concerns failures of communication; patients feel that doctors fail to supply them with adequate information about their condition and its management. Doctors most commonly express discontent about the failure of their patients to carry out the advice or treatment recommended. There can be few doctors who are at a loss for spectacular examples of patients who do not comply with their instructions—diabetics who forget to take their insulin and thereby risk death, bronchitic patients who continue to smoke. It is when doctors are dismayed by this apparently inexplicable behaviour that the psychologists' task begins. As yet, they have little to offer in the way of direct advice but they do possess a theory and methodology for studying human behaviour which enables them to undertake the task. As we shall see, there is evidence that patient cooperation is enhanced by a good personal relationship with the doctor. Psychologists can explore ways of establishing and maintaining satisfying and effective patient–doctor relationships. Attention should also be paid to the nature and causes of poor relationships, with a view to improving them. In this chapter we shall examine selected aspects of the relation between doctor and patient (including communications) from a mainly psychological point of view. We shall also discuss some proposed remedies and suggest some lines of development.

There is evidence that many patients are unable to recall the greater part of what their doctor tells them in their consultation, within minutes of seeing him.[3] As a result of this many patients fail to act on the doctor's orders. One of us had a vivid demonstration of this disarming fact a few years ago when he was a patient in a surgical ward. Each evening the medicine trolley was rolled into the ward by at least two nurses who carefully supervised the correct allocation of drugs to each patient. They went to great lengths to check and countercheck the delivery of each tablet, which was meticulously recorded in a duty book. For the most part the patients accepted the tablets with apparent gratitude. Shortly after the nurses trundled their trolley along to the next ward, many of the patients who were able to get up, usually at least half the number on the ward, would retire to the bathrooms and surreptitiously or ceremoniously, depending on individual personality styles, flush the tablets down the lavatory.

It has not come as a total surprise therefore to learn from Ley that 48·7 per cent of patients fail to take their antibiotic tablets, 37·5 per cent fail to take their anti-tuberculosis drugs, and so on.[2] To make matters worse, some studies of out-patients have shown that even among those patients who attempt to comply with doctor's orders anything from one-quarter to two-thirds may be taking the wrong dose and up to 30 per cent are making errors which are potentially dangerous. A striking example of the barriers which sometimes exist between doctor and patient is described by Fletcher,[4] who quotes a colleague as estimating that '80 per cent of dying patients know that they are dying and would wish to talk about it and 80 per cent of doctors deny this and believe that patients should not be told' [p. 29].[4] This estimate is consistent with the few available attitude surveys, from which it emerges that members of the medical profession generally are of the opinion that most patients do not wish to be told if and when they have a fatal condition. Patients on the other hand express a desire to be told the worst. It appears that the argument for keeping patients in ignorance, on the grounds that they only wish to hear good news, may be unfounded. Aitken-Swan and Easson, for example, informed 231 of their patients when they had cancer and only 7 per cent of them subsequently said that they would rather not have known.[5] This important and extremely sensitive subject calls for full, careful and urgent psychological research.

In a survey carried out in 1960, no less than two-thirds of discharged patients expressed dissatisfaction with the communications in the hospital. In other surveys, including some carried out in well-staffed teaching hospitals, this proportion is slightly lower (between 30 per cent and 60 per cent) but still unacceptably high. Ley and Spelman point out that dissatisfaction with communications (usually complaints of receiving inadequate information about their problems and treatment) is the most frequent criticism made by patients.[2, 6] They add that improved communications can reduce stress and also improve the patient's contribution to his own treatment, for instance by keeping to the prescribed diet, carrying out required exercises, actually taking the pills which are prescribed, and so on. It has been suggested that a major reason for this dissatisfaction is the decline of the traditional system of medicine which centred on the establishment of a familar and trusting relationship with a single family doctor.[1] As this system is replaced by short consultations with unfamiliar doctors, the opportunity for establishing such a relationship is precluded. In the shift from a familiar and comforting figure to a highly trained and technically more competent specialist in medicine, we are in danger of overlooking the considerable part played by psychological factors in ensuring accurate and satisfactory communications between doctor and patient and, as a by-product of this communication, satisfactory compliance with the prescribed course of action.

In an attempt to come to grips with some aspects of the communication between doctor and patient and its relation to the successful practice of medicine, Korsch and Negrete have been carrying out interesting research at a children's hospital in Los Angeles. The greatest part of their research has been carried out in an emergency paediatric clinic staffed by highly trained young doctors with between one to three years of paediatric experience. The visits are usually short and generally result in a specific recommendation from the doctor to the parent. The usual reason for the emergency visit is an acute but generally minor illness. In their major study they observed the visits of eight hundred different patients (i.e. parent and child), and interviewed the mother in each case. Most of the interviews were tape-recorded; the mother was questioned immediately after each consultation and then again fourteen days later to ascertain whether she had carried out the doctor's advice. The information from this major study was supplemented by observations made in general practice, healthy baby clinics and the like.

The most reassuring finding to emerge from the major study was that three-quarters of the mothers were satisfied with the doctors' performance in their brief consultation. Despite this general satisfaction, however, there are grounds for concern as nearly half the mothers were unclear about what had caused their child's illness. The importance of this finding is that many of the mothers assumed incorrectly that they might have been negligent and this was an unnecessary source of distress for them. Moreover, only 42 per cent of the mothers carried out all the doctor's advice, 11 per cent did not comply at all and one-third carried out part of the instructions only (for the remaining 14 per cent data was unobtainable). As might be expected, there was a close association between the mother's satisfaction with the consultation and the extent to which she carried out the doctor's advice. Rather surprisingly, however, there was no correlation between the duration of the consultation and the amount of satisfaction expressed by the mother, or between the duration of the consultation and the clarity of the diagnosis offered to the mother.

Among the specific complaints levelled by the mothers was a lack of interest shown by the doctor, the excessive use of jargon which was often misunderstood (for instance, 'lumbar puncture' gave rise to misunderstandings) and a lack of empathy with the anxious mothers. It was also found that the doctors talked more than the mothers and that only 5 per cent of the doctors' conversation was personal or friendly. The main findings of Korsch and Negrete can be summarised:

Friendly treatment of the patient (i.e. the mother) generally had favourable results: harsh treatment tended to yield poor results. And there was a direct statistical relation between the amount of non-medical (that is, sociable) conversation between doctor and patient and the patient's satisfaction with the encounter with the doctor [p. 74].[1]

26

The importance of these findings is twofold. In the first place they show how easy it is to provide comfort for the anxious mother of a sick child and, equally, how easy it is to ignore this most obvious need. Secondly, these research workers were able to demonstrate a close relationship between the mother's satisfaction with the consultation and the extent to which she carried out prescribed treatment.

We shall give one closing observation from this American study. As the quotation above shows, the friendliness expressed by the doctor makes a valuable contribution to the mother's satisfaction. Most of the doctors believed that they had been friendly, but less than half of the patients shared this impression. It is on differences of perception and impression such as these that deep and lasting misunderstandings are built and sustained.

Further evidence of the failure of patients to carry out their doctor's advice can easily be found. In those studies where checks have been carried out (by laboratory tests, the use of external informants, and so on) it is found that patients ignore a surprising amount of medical advice. For example, in a study quoted by Ley and Spelman no fewer than twenty-seven out of fifty diabetic patients failed to take their prescribed insulin regularly and correctly.[6] The finding that up to 50 per cent of patients may fail to take their prescribed drugs has also been reported for ulcer patients, psychiatric patients (failure to take drugs is a major cause of relapse in schizophrenia) and other groups. Furthermore, general advice such as the use of diets, relaxation classes, vitamins for babies and so on has been reported to be followed by fewer than half the patients concerned. In a treatment study of the effects of a psychological method on the occurrence of bed-wetting at night among children living in a poor area, no fewer than thirty-nine out of eighty-one mothers failed to carry out the necessary procedures.[7] This disappointingly high failure-rate occurred despite the deliberate exclusion from treatment of children whose parents seemed on first interview to be unable or unwilling to comply with the requirements of the treatment regime, and despite our provision of a full explanation and demonstration of what was required. It is interesting to note that the failure of parents to carry out the treatment programme was significantly reduced when the children concerned were given tablets to take. The parental failure-rate in cases where tablets were not given was 30 per cent, but only 12 per cent with a stimulant tablet.

Like earlier investigators, Ley and Spelman found evidence of misconceptions about medical matters in a lay population but they were rather less extensive and serious than might have been feared.[6] Certainly lay knowledge was greater than predicted by a sample of doctors—in an American study it was shown that 81 per cent of a sample of doctors underestimated their patients' knowledge. Moreover, the doctors were inclined to give the least information to their worst-informed patients.

Assessing how much of the information and advice given by doctors was recalled by their patients, Ley and Spelman found that a good deal, roughly one-third, was forgotten promptly. Fortunately, the most important bits of information were generally the best-recalled. Notable exceptions have been encountered, however, in which patients forgot the diagnosis, even of a serious illness, within a few weeks of being informed. The same workers have also found that patients who have a good knowledge of medical matters recall better than ignorant ones, and an anxious patient finds it more difficult to recall the doctor's information and advice.

On the other hand, neither age nor intelligence were related to the degree of forgetfulness. Another interesting finding, which would bear considerable development, is that a patient's satisfaction varies with his mood. It was found that when there was little depression (on discharge from hospital) satisfaction was fairly high. When the patient became more depressed between two and four weeks after discharge, satisfaction correspondingly declined. Lastly, when depression lessened again in the eighth week, satisfaction once again increased.

Ley and his colleagues have not been content with mere identification and description of inadequate communication, but have also attempted to improve the quality and durability of the communications. Some of their preliminary findings suggest that the patient could more accurately recall the doctor's information if the doctor gave the most important information first and emphasised the few most important aspects of it.[8] Recall was also made easier when the doctor presented the information in a logical sequence, for instance, 'This is what is wrong with you, this is what we will do, this is what will happen, this is what treatment you need, and this is what you must do to help yourself.' They have also found that extra visits by the doctor increased the patient's understanding and, ultimately, his compliance.

Other suggestions which might be worth taking up include the use of memory aids in the form of written material, as well as, or instead of, conveying the essential information to at least one other person, such as a close relative. From research of Korsch and Negrete in California, the lesson seems to be that we need to assist doctors in achieving a friendly manner which will increase the satisfaction of the patient and thereby improve his compliance. There is a considerable psychological literature on the persuasive effects of various forms of communication, briefly described on page 33 below, that can be used in improving doctor–patient and patient–doctor interactions.

Communicating with doctors

So far attention has been paid almost exclusively to the failure of doctors to communicate adequately with their patients. This attention is not misplaced because, as we have already seen, this is the most common complaint levelled by patients at the medical care which they receive. This should not, however, obscure the failures of communication in the other direction—that is, from patient to doctor. There is some evidence that failure of communication underlies the most common complaint reported by the *doctors*. As we have seen, they feel that far too many of their patients fail to co-operate in carrying out the advice and instructions given to them. In our view there is another important cause of dissatisfaction among doctors that seems so far to have escaped attention.

Most psychologists would agree that the consequences of a particular form of behaviour play a major part in determining whether the behaviour will be modified. If the consequences of behaviour are unknown, obscure or infrequently observed, it is far less likely that that behaviour will change. This can be stated more positively: the provision of prompt and accurate information about the consequences of our behaviour will facilitate learning and improvements. In many situations in medicine, particularly general practice, feedback of this type is, at best, irregularly provided. Doctors in general practice seldom see the best results of their work, as the patients who recover or are otherwise satisfied are *not* the ones who return for further consultations. This means that for the most part a general practitioner receives little reward for his efforts; he has to deduce from the fact that his patient does not turn up again in the waiting-room that his advice or treatment has been successful. On the other hand, the failure of a course of treatment is more likely to be brought to his notice. In other words, doctors receive frequent reminders of failure and infrequent acknowledgements of success. It seems likely to us that this situation will produce adverse results, as it is bound to be demoralising for many doctors. If a psychologist set out deliberately to design a programme of persistent punishment he would need to add little to the existing system under which most general practitioners function.

In addition to the emotional effects of exposure to a punishing 'learning' situation of this type, the erratic and unbalanced flow of information coming back to the doctor from his patients provides ideal conditions for inducing behavioural changes of the wrong type. Successful actions on the doctor's part are rarely and irregularly reinforced. Ineffective actions on the other hand are regularly 'punished' (by the repeated returns of the dissatisfied patients), and the doctor can only hope that the fact that a patient does not return means that he is cured. As we know, however, a high proportion of patients who feel dissatisfied with a particular piece of advice or recommended treatment will avoid telling their doctors. Instead they go elsewhere, try self-medication or seek non-medical assistance.

In this muddled situation the doctor's dilemma can be put in this way: if one of his patients fails to return for a second consultation after he has prescribed a course of therapeutic action, one of three conclusions is possible. The therapy may have been effective and there is therefore no need for the patient to return; the therapy may have been ineffective but the patient does not request a second consultation because he has sought help elsewhere; or the patient did not act on the advice anyway—either because he failed to understand the instruction or because, understanding it, he decided not to carry out the doctor's suggestion.

Let us translate this into a hypothetical example of a general practitioner who, in the course of one month, is consulted by ten patients suffering from stomach ulcers. In each of the ten cases he recommends that they take a prescribed drug three times daily and, in addition, that they should keep to a special diet, the details of which are provided. Within a month three of the patients return to complain that they have had no relief. How is this outcome to be interpreted? Does it mean that the course of treatment recommended is effective in the majority of cases? Strictly speaking, all that the doctor could conclude is that it is ineffective in a minority of cases and has unknown effects in the majority of cases.

The seven patients who do not seek a second consultation may have derived considerable benefit from the treatment, or they may have sought help elsewhere, or they may have decided not to take the tablets nor to keep to the prescribed diet. It is easy to see how a general practitioner forced to rely solely on his own clinical experience would be compelled to make decisions on the basis of 'systematic chaos'. Fortunately for everyone concerned, this is not the only source of information available to doctors. The position is, and it will certainly remain so in the future, that they have recourse to information obtained in other settings, in a systematic and controlled manner.

It is easy, however, to think of simple expedients to improve the flow of information back to the doctor. Although some of the problems seem to be almost insurmountable (such as ascertaining the reliability of some of the information), the introduction of a regular feedback system by means of telephone calls, postcards or reports from health visitors would be a useful improvement. For obvious reasons the return flow of information is far greater in most hospitals (for instance, the opportunity for repeated and prolonged observations), but even here a substantial amount of valuable *psychological* information is lost—simply for lack of trying.

We look forward to psychological investigations designed to improve the flow of information to the doctor and to assess the effect of this information on his level of satisfaction and effectiveness.

Persuasive communications

Although there are endless stories about patients, even seriously ill ones, who ignore the clear warnings given to them by their doctors, there is some encouraging evidence to show that a well-timed and forceful piece of advice from a GP can be extremely effective. To take one example, Williams states that 37 per cent of patients with chest complaints gave up smoking when strongly advised to do so by their medical practitioner.[9] As far as we can tell at present, many people do respond to warnings about their health. We also know that in many circumstances a more alarming message is more effective in changing people's attitudes. Unfortunately changes of attitude obtained in this way do not necessarily lead to action. When even messages that arouse considerable fear fail to persuade, it often means that the recipient is unable to take appropriate action. The best combination seems to be a fear-evoking message followed by instructions which make it easier for the appropriate action to be taken. For example, Leventhal found that one in three of his subjects took an anti-tetanus shot after receiving a fear-provoking warning combined with specific action instructions which were easy to carry out. When the action instructions were omitted, however, only one in thirty people took the appropriate steps.[10]

In an influential early study of this topic it was found that a low-fear message was more effective than a high-fear message.[11] School-children were first instructed in dental care and then given either high, low or moderately fear-provoking information about the dangers of inadequate dental care. The pupils who received a high-fear message showed least improvement in caring for their teeth. For some time psychologists thought that this apparent greater effectiveness of low-fear messages might be generally the case. Later findings have shown, however, that in many instances a high-fear message is in fact more effective—at the very least, for changing attitudes, if not always for inducing a change in behaviour. For example, Leventhal and his colleagues reported some success in using a fear-provoking film of an operation to remove a lung cancer in changing the attitudes of a group of smokers.[12] They also observed a slight tendency for patients who saw this film to act on the recommendation that, as smokers, they should take advantage of the easy facilities for obtaining a chest X-ray. In a second group of smokers, comparable improvements in attitude and action were achieved by a less frightening version of the same film. A third group of smokers who received similar background information to the first two groups but did not see the film showed less attitude change and fewer of them took advantage of the X-ray service. So, in this instance at least, a fear-provoking appeal brought about the desired change in attitude and, to a lesser degree, the desired action.

In this study there was a weak relationship between the change in attitude and effective action. This poor correspondence between attitude change and behavioural change has been reported on a number of occasions.[13] Even when high-fear-provoking messages are more successful in changing attitudes, it has been found that considerably less alarming messages are just as successful in producing changes in *behaviour*. So, for example, it has been found that alarming messages about the dangers of smoking produce greater changes in attitude; but, despite this, the reduction in actual smoking is similar for groups receiving messages which provoke high or low levels of fear. Similar findings have been reported by psychologists attempting to persuade people to undergo anti-tetanus injections. Despite the more favourable attitudes induced by fear-provoking messages, there was no difference between the high- or low-fear groups in the numbers of those who obtained the injection.

It should be remembered that frightening messages can be ineffective. It has been suggested that in medical matters a failure to act on the advice given in an alarming message may arise from the possibility that the action proposed is itself painful or distressing. So, heavy smokers may fail to undergo the recommended X-ray because they are aware that a positive finding might lead to chest surgery; a positive X-ray diagnosis of tuberculosis may lead to protracted treatment in hospital, and so on.

Psychologists are also beginning to show an interest in individual differences in response to health-care messages; it seems likely that people with low self-esteem may be less likely to act on recommended diagnostic or treatment procedures, particularly if frightening messages are used. Fear-producing warnings may reinforce their sense of hopelessness and the belief that the dangers cannot successfully be avoided. For people with low self-esteem it may be preferable to use messages that produce little fear and contain clear, specific, simple instructions for taking appropriate action. Let us take an hypothetical example. Among sufferers from venereal disease, those who have low self-esteem will be more likely to seek treatment if given a mildly fearful warning coupled with specific and simple advice about how and where to obtain treatment. Care should be taken to emphasise that the treatment is generally brief and painless, as it usually is. As recommendations for treatment have been shown to be more persuasive if they are described as being highly effective, it should also be pointed out to VD sufferers that current methods are in fact extremely successful. Lastly, it is probably wise to avoid using alarming warnings when dealing with people who already have feelings of hopelessness (such as those encountered particularly in psychiatric practice). Recent research has confirmed that hopelessness is one of the most prominent psychological states present in people who attempt to commit suicide.

3 Pain

Despite the universality and importance of painful experiences, clinical psychologists have neglected the subject. Instead, many of them still spend much of their working lives puzzling over the mysteries of what their psychiatrically disturbed subjects perceive in ink-blots. This imbalance, which is, of course, one of the less fortunate consequences of psychologists' over-concern with abnormal behaviour, is a matter for particular regret because of the importance of psychological factors in pain. Moreover, one of the most influential of contemporary theories of pain was proposed jointly by a psychologist, R. Melzack, and physiologist, P. Wall.

Part of the explanation for psychologists' neglect of the subject can be traced to the fact that many of them share the widespread belief that pain experiences are determined solely by direct physical causes—burns, breaks, cuts, systemic dysfunctions, and so on. Psychological factors, it is conceded, are relevant but insignificant. This view reflects a conception of pain which is outdated.

Another reason for the neglect of pain research is the belief that pain, a secondary phenomenon, is of little interest in its own right. As Melzack points out in his valuable book, *The Puzzle of Pain*, 'research time and money is devoted to many problems of obvious clinical significance, but pain, often considered the symptom and not the disease, receives far less attention' [p. 203].[1]

Our main aims in this chapter are to draw attention to the new conception of pain, the role of psychological factors in pain and to indicate some of the ways in which psychologists can contribute to an increased understanding of pain and how to modify it. The extent of the opportunities can be illustrated by two simple facts. Complaints of pain are an extremely common reason for seeking medical advice, and psychological factors exert a major influence on pain experiences. The question is whether clinical psychologists have anything practical to contribute.

The view that pain is always and necessarily a consequence (and indeed a symptom) of injury or physical illness is not entirely accurate. It is now evident that people without known organic pathology suffer pain, the validity of which cannot be doubted. Secondly, even when an organic basis for pain is established, psychological factors continue to affect the experience of pain (for instance, its quality, intensity and duration). Then there are those extraordinary examples of people who experience little or no pain despite severe injuries. It is common knowledge that, during religious ceremonies but not at other times, dervishes are capable of enduring what would otherwise be extremely painful stimulation with apparent tranquillity. Anyone who has seen them pierce both cheeks with a sharp metal skewer, apparently painlessly, can never doubt the paramount importance of psychological factors.

Another striking example of the influence of such factors comes from a study reported by Beecher. He found that 35 out of 100 surgical patients experienced relief from pain after receiving a placebo when they were expecting morphine.[2] Their strong expectation that the pain would be helped by the supposed injection of morphine was sufficient to bring relief.

Pain

The inadequacy of a conception of pain based on a direct one-to-one relationship between sensory input (for instance, tissue injury) and pain experience is obvious in cases of self-mutilation. Some psychologically disturbed patients, usually young women with personality disorders, deliberately and repeatedly injure themselves. The most common form of self-mutilation is cutting—of the face and arms. Characteristically, these patients report no pain when inflicting the injuries, even though these are often severe. Instead they describe feelings of relief and a decrease in tension. One of our patients, a seventeen-year-old girl, who repeatedly slashed her face (causing serious disfigurement), said that she experienced no pain from the injuries, although she was normally sensitive to pain incurred in other circumstances. Her explanation for this behaviour was that feelings of unhappiness and a numb tension built up in her until they became intolerable, and she had learned that she could achieve rapid release from this tension by cutting herself. A period of relative calm then followed and she felt no pain from her wounds. In this, as in many other cases of self-injury, there was no relationship between the severity of the damage and the pain experience.

The concept of pain

Neglect of a psychological approach to the suffering of people in pain derives mainly from the long-established belief that the experience of pain is directly related to the amount of bodily damage or, exceptionally, to the intensity of stimulation. According to this view the suffering results from and is proportional to the extent of the damage sustained; acceptance of this view leads to attempts to reduce the feedback of bodily damage

to the central processing centres (for instance, by healing the damage or severing connecting fibres). Underlying these views is the specificity theory of pain proposed by von Frey, a German physiologist who worked
at the universities of Leipzig and Wurzburg at the turn
of the century. In summary, he postulated the existence
of specific pain receptors in body tissue which transmit
distress messages directly to a pain centre in the brain.
He conceived of a relay system operating like a direct
telephone link from the periphery to a central exchange,
sometimes called the push-button theory. It is now
agreed however that there are a number of pieces of
clinical evidence that refute the direct-line relay model
of the nervous system.[1] Firstly, it has been shown
that surgical interventions in the peripheral or
central nervous system do not reliably produce permanent abolition of pain (e.g. cutting a peripheral
nerve supply). According to the von Frey theory,
if the distress messages are prevented from reaching
the pain centre no pain should be felt. Thus
studies in which surgical intervention has not reduced
pain satisfactorily run contrary to the specificity theory.
Secondly, the theory cannot explain the occurrence of
phantom limb pain, causalgia and neuralgias. Phantom
limb pain is a bizarre and distressing syndrome that
occurs in approximately 35 per cent of people who
have had a limb amputated. The pain is usually felt
as if it was located in the limb that has actually been
lost—or the sufferer may report bizarre feelings, for
example that the fingers of his amputated hand are
digging continuously into his palm. In about 5 per
cent of these cases the phantom pain persists in a severe
form and may even worsen with time.

Livingstone reported a case of a physician who had
had his arm amputated after being wounded by a

pointed instrument (puncture wound).[3] 'Not infrequently he had a sensation as if a sharp scalpel was being driven repeatedly, deep into the site of his original puncture wound . . . In intervals between the sharper attacks of pain he experienced a persistent burning in the hand.' Causalgias and neuralgias are pains that persist long after the occurrence of injuries to the peripheral nervous system and certainly long after the tissues have been repaired. Lastly, pain is sometimes experienced in one part of the body after stimulation of an unrelated, non-pathological part of the body. (The interesting story of the development of von Frey's theory from three strands of evidence is well described and evaluated in Melzack's book.)

Not all von Frey's assumptions have stood up to examination. One of the weakest parts of his theory is the assumption that the intensity of stimulation is in direct proportion to the perception of pain. The quality of the pain, its intensity and its tolerability are influenced by a number of psychological variables which interact with the stimulation arising from the physical damage.

Before elaborating on these psychological determinants we need to consider some valuable observations by Beecher.[2] He made the surprising claim that only about one-third of the severely wounded soldiers taken to hospital from a battlefield requested pain-killers; the majority either denied that they felt any pain or believed it to be too minor to require medication—despite their serious injuries. He notes that these soldiers were not suffering from shock and that they complained about injections as would any other patient. Beecher then compared the behaviour of the combat group to that of a group of male civilian patients undergoing major surgery and thereby sustaining tissue injury, although of a less severe kind than that experienced by the soldiers. In the civilian group, four out of five patients requested medication to relieve their pain. He concluded that 'the pain is in very large part determined by other factors, and of great importance here is the significance of the wound, i.e. reaction to the wound' [p. 165].

Beecher's observations and others of a similar character make plain some important weaknesses of specificity theory—the omission of psychological contributors to pain experience and the unsupported assumption of a direct relationship between tissue injury and pain. It is now evident that sensory stimulation, regarded as the single basis for pain in earlier theories, must take its place as the principal but not the sole factor in a complex experience. Among the psychological factors contributing to the experience are attitudes, beliefs, cultural views, moods such as anxiety and depression, focus of attention, motivation and personality traits. We have now to deal with the many and interacting factors that cause pain and focus interest on the functional relationships between them. A pain over the heart may be intense and produce great suffering in someone unaware that it is probably due to indigestion. Another person, aware of the signs and significance of indigestion, is likely to regard the same pain as being weak and to be ignored. With the onset of his supposed 'heart pain', the first sufferer will no longer notice a toothache that has been nagging at him. Simple examples of this type illustrate how one's attention to and interpretation of the significance of a pain can affect its quality and intensity.

A theory that has tried to come to grips with this more complex view of pain is that proposed by Melzack[1] and Wall—the gate theory, which postulates a mechanism that exercises selective control of stimulation. Without going into the intricacies of their position, it can be said that it appears to explain a number of findings regarding the recognition and coding of sensory information, while strongly implicating psychological processes in the perception of pain. They have suggested that a strong influence is exerted by the brain on the transmission of information along the spinal cord. According to this hypothesis, messages coming from the periphery along the cord can be changed by messages moving downwards from the brain. These downward influences include cognitive and other psychological factors (such as attention, anxiety and anticipation). The effects of such psychological variables are felt before the peripheral messages reach the brain. Although much more elaboration of how these influences operate is required, the inclusion of powerful downward influences is a useful expansion of the theory of pain. Among other advantages, it provides a framework for the introduction of those central factors which are known to play an important part in pain perception.

Psychological factors

The factors of attention, suggestion, anxiety and anticipation are known to have a significant effect on pain experiences; for instance, it is commonly observed that a minor injury sustained during some absorbing activity such as a game of football passes unnoticed. A standard injection given to a woman just as her baby is born (to aid detachment of the afterbirth) is seldom felt. Similar experiences can be reproduced in experiments in which the subject's attention is diverted during exposure to painful stimulation.

A complex set of psychological phenomena which are usually summarised (rather unsatisfactorily) by the term 'suggestion' certainly influence pain. Given the appropriate suggestion, hypnotised people report little or no pain from cuts and burns. Yogis in states of self-induced hypnosis or meditation readily carry out normally painful acts without evident pain. Reference has already been made to dervishes who put skewers through their cheeks. Some years ago one of us was able to observe an Indian religious ceremony in which devoted men, after a prolonged preparation of rhythmic chanting and dancing, walked along a path of glowing coals, without pain—or rather without complaint of pain. Nor did they show overt signs of having undergone a painful experience.

In all these examples there is a strong element of suggestion operating, either self-suggestion or suggestion provided by others. In an experiment conducted to investigate the efficiency of intense auditory stimulation in reducing pain (audio-analgesia), Melzack and his colleagues obtained clear evidence of the role of suggestion in pain tolerance.[4] For experimental purposes they used artificially produced pain induced by the cold pressor test, in which the participants immerse their hands in an ice bath, which produces a deep, slow-rising pain. Three groups of people were used. One group received intense auditory stimulation as a pain-reducer. The second group received the same auditory stimulation as well as a strong suggestion enhancing the value of this stimulation as a means of diminishing pain. The third group were told that ultrasonic sounds are powerful pain-reducers, but then received only a low hum throughout the experimental period. The results showed that the participants who received intense auditory stimulation coupled with strong suggestion were able to keep their hands in the water significantly longer than those from either of the other two groups. The intense auditory stimulation alone did not raise pain tolerance; only when it was combined with the forceful influence of suggestion were satisfactory results achieved. A practical application of these and similar findings was made in the field of dentistry. Numbers of dentists, especially in the United States, installed earphones for their patients and allowed them to listen to music throughout their treatment. Unfortunately, the full significance of the accompanying suggestions was not widely known or appreciated and they were neglected by many of the dentists. Consequently, although many patients benefited from this form of pain reduction, considerable disappointment was also reported and, overall, the use of traditional analgesics in dentistry does not appear to have been greatly reduced.

Although it is premature to offer definitive statements, some evidence indicates that the procedure used in acupuncture for eliminating or reducing pain depends heavily on suggestions given by a firm believer in acupuncture to a suggestible patient. Based on Chinese traditional medicine, the procedure is capable of producing analgesia without the use of drugs. Needles are applied to particular parts of the body and this results in a dulling or elimination of pain, either in the same part or in areas far from the location of the needles. The patient remains conscious throughout and is capable of conversing or even taking refreshment. According to Cheng and Ding,[5] it appears to work best on short operations and only on certain types of patient: 'the success of the use of acupuncture analgesia depends on the willingness and understanding of the patients'. They therefore select emotionally stable, intelligent individuals who are confident about the advantages of acupuncture. There can be few people, and certainly very few psychologists, who find no interest in this intriguing phenomenon.

Anxiety can have a considerable effect on both the quality and intensity of pain experiences. Patients who are anxious are more sensitive to pain and, as might be predicted from this, neurotic patients (who generally have high levels of anxiety) complain of pain more than others.[6] Leucotomy (a brain operation in which fibres joining the front section of the brain to the mid-brain are severed), performed for the relief of pain, produces the best results in those patients whose anxiety is also markedly reduced by the operation. However, it appears that the operation alters rather than eliminates pain experiences. The pain is found to be less intrusive and less incapacitating, and in this sense can be said to be less distressing.

It has been estimated that 75 per cent of post-surgical patients obtain marked relief from morphine. But, as we have seen, Beecher found that in many cases pain was greatly relieved after the administration of a placebo instead of the usual morphine.[2] Recalling Beecher's observations on wounded soldiers who needed far less treatment by analgesics than did hospital patients undergoing voluntary surgery, it seems certain that these two groups had different attitudes towards their injuries. The soldiers, after a period of stress in combat, found themselves alive and safe in a quiet ward. The voluntary patients, awakening in a ward and having varied expectations concerning the success of the operation and the pain and discomfort, would regard their surgical injuries very differently from battle wounds. The context and significance of the wound appear to have a considerable effect on how much pain is suffered and reported. The concept of pain complaint, and its relation to pain experience, are interesting subjects but difficult to come to grips with simply because much of our information about pain experience is derived from pain complaints; hence it is difficult to disentangle the two. We can be sure, however, that it is unwise to regard pain experience and pain complaints as being synonymous.

We need to bear in mind the cultural factors which enter into the style and frequency of complaining. For example, it is commonly observed that women make more pain complaints than men. This sex difference probably reflects the prevailing view of acceptable masculine behaviour. Men are expected to complain less and endure more. Views and expectations of this sort also influence the behaviour of doctors and nurses. For example, Bond and Pilowsky found that analgesics were often given by nurses in a way that was not consistent with the patient's own assessment of his pain or with his request for relief.[7] Women were given more powerful analgesics for less severe pain than were men, whose requests for relief were often ignored by the nursing staff. The influence of cultural factors is also seen in the variations of pain tolerance across different groups during similar experiences, such as childbirth. In his experiments, Hardy found a cultural variation; levels of radiant heat said by North Europeans to be merely warm evoked a different reaction from people of Mediterranean origin, who complained that they were painful.[8]

Valuable evidence on differences in pain tolerance was accumulated on a massive sample of 41,000 people tested at Stanford University. Woodrow and his colleagues found that men tolerate more pain than women, whites more than blacks and blacks more than Asians. Pain tolerance decreased with age.[9]

Other psychological factors in pain experiences are the predictability of the pain and the possibility of exerting some control over it. In experimental work it has been shown that electric shocks are more bearable when the person can predict when or how strongly they will occur; sometimes he is given both these facts. The results of Janis (see Chapter 10), who found that patients had less post-operative pain when adequately informed and prepared, may be partly an outcome of this factor of predictability.[10] Some interesting experimental work in which variations in tolerance for pain were produced by preparing participants for painful experiences is consistent with this notion. 'Rehearsals' of the anticipated pain have been found to increase tolerance, and the more similar the rehearsed experienced is to the pain to be experienced, the greater the increase in tolerance.

Personality differences have also been shown to affect complaining. Bond studied fifty-two women with carcinoma of the cervix to see how their personality traits and attitudes to the disease related to the pain they felt and their complaints.[11] He found that pain-free patients were less emotional and more sociable, while patients experiencing pain but not complaining of it were emotional but not sociable. Finally, the patients who were both emotional and sociable experienced and complained of considerable pain, thereby receiving more medication. Bond suggests that personality characteristics of this type may help to explain the reluctance of some patients to consult their doctors, despite the onset of serious illness. It may also help to explain the varied success which different individuals have in obtaining treatment, including analgesics, from their doctors.

Personality differences are related to pain tolerance

as well as complaint. Lynn and Eysenck used a thermo-stimulator technique, involving the application of steadily increasing degrees of heat, to assess pain toler-ance in a group of students.[12] When they were divided on the basis of their personality scores, pain toler-ance was found to increase with extraversion. On the other hand, introverts appeared to be more sensitive to painful stimulation. In related work, Sybil Eysenck in-vestigated differences in pain experience during child-birth and concluded that personality differences affect not only the quality but also the intensity of the pain experienced.[13] As with the results obtained from students, she found that introverts, in contrast to extra-verts, appeared to feel pain sooner and more intensely but to complain less, although they might remember the pain more vividly afterwards. Petrie has also con-tributed some interesting investigations in the field of in-dividual differences.[14] She suggests that people can be grouped into two types on the basis of a test of kinaes-thetic after-effects in which the persisting effects of stimulation are assessed. 'Augmenters' appear to over-estimate sensory input while 'reducers' diminish input. The results of these two groups on kinaesthetic tests cor-related significantly with their personality scores and with differences in pain tolerance. She found that re-ducers had higher extraversion scores and greater toler-ance of pain. Replication and development of her findings might well improve our understanding of the relationship between personality, pain tolerance and complaints of pain (see Eysenck's theory[15]).

In addition to anxiety, it seems likely that moods, such as depression or elation, the degree of alertness and physical fatigue, will prove to be important factors in pain experience.

Beecher was so convinced of the importance of psychological factors in determining what he called the 're-action component of pain' that he came to regard laboratory (and hence, artificial) investigations of pain as being virtually useless.[2] The significance of the injury, its importance in the person's life, his view of the situation in which the injury was sustained, the anxiety induced by the injury, and so on, cannot be adequately reproduced in the predictable conditions of a laboratory. He felt that these omissions would invalidate the research. Although his dismissal is too sweeping, some support for his view comes from the finding that analgesics which in clinical practice are completely reliable give variable results in experimentally induced pain. An important factor in the clinical effectiveness of these drugs is their psychological significance in the setting of hospital or surgery and the positive attitude of the doctor.

It is hard to escape the view that pain is a complex phenomenon dependent on sensory input and a number of psychological factors. The extent of the interaction between these two types of determinants has not been unravelled and is an inviting challenge for psychologists. Progress in clarifying these relationships would be a useful step towards a more practical approach in applying psychological expertise to the modification of pain.

> Some of the most unbearable pains, such as cardiac pain, rise so rapidly in intensity that the patient is unable to achieve any control over them. On the other hand, some slowly rising temporal pains are susceptible to central control and may allow the person to think about something else or use other strategems to keep the pain under control. [p. 200].[1]

It seems evident that psychologists would do well to tackle these slowly rising pains first.

General implications

What implications can be drawn from these observations of pain experience and behaviour? Firstly, we need to adopt a broader approach to the relief of pain. Many of the factors which affect experiences of pain are either neglected or manipulated in ignorance by people who confine their attention to the physical determinants of pain—as conceived in von Frey's specificity theory. Over fifteen years ago Beecher felt that there was sufficient evidence already available 'to lead future therapeutic research into the modification of the psychic reaction to the original sensation' [p. 189]. Despite the fact that Beecher's views have been extensively quoted over the intervening years, the medical and ancillary professions, showing few signs of acknowledging the extra-physical components of pain, continue to treat it as if it was a simple and direct reflection of sensory disturbances. Patients still complain that many doctors do not seem prepared to take the time to allay their anxiety by adequate explanations of their pain, or to give them details of impending painful events such as operations (see Chapter 10). Few systematic attempts have been made to employ specific psychological procedures to reduce pain. Instead we continue to rely almost exclusively on analgesic drugs and, in extreme cases, surgery.

Practical implications

As a step towards improvement in the psychological management of pain, we propose eight modification procedures which might be of some practical value.

1 Fully informing patients of expected discomforts from operations, deteriorating diseases and so on. Speci-

fic instructions concerning the type of pain that can be predicted to occur during the course of an illness, following an operation, in childbirth and so on. Information should deal with the intensity of the pain, its location, quality, duration, likelihood of secondary discomforts (such as indigestion and urinary discomfort). If this were done, the patient would encounter few unexpected (and hence potentially frightening), unpleasant sensations and by comprehending, almost certainly cope better with his symptoms and their side-effects.

2   The use of desensitisation (see Chapter 9) and specific anxiety-reduction techniques (already available in psychology) to deal with cases where the significance of the symptom or illness produces an unreasonable degree of fear.

3   The deliberate and systematic use of suggestion as an aid in speeding recovery, reducing the intensity of the pain and so on.

4   As distraction can help in the attenuation of pain it would be of interest to assess the usefulness of developing a set of routines for patients that would enable them to turn their concern and attention away from the symptom or painful part.

5   Teaching of self-control procedures (see Chapter 7) for the reduction of specific symptoms (such as specific muscular relaxation for secondary symptoms such as headache).

6   Instructions designed to improve the detection by the patient of his need for further medication, thereby increasing self-control and prediction.

7   Social attention and other rewards can be given, contingent on the reduction of complaints of pain—especially relevant in cases of chronic pain problems. Praise and attention are promptly given for statements and actions indicating improvements.

8   In cases of self-mutilation, it may prove necessary to turn all these methods upside-down. If we reformulate the problem raised by these patients, we can think of a new aim for treatment—by regarding the problem as one of *lowering* their pain-thresholds, we might then consider ways of elevating their anxiety, focusing full attention on the wound, rewarding them by increased attention when they make pain complaints and so on. Obviously these possibilities will need to be explored with great care.

Having entered the field so late, psychologists are faced with a host of tasks and problems and many of them will need to specialise in the study of pain. Melzack goes so far as to recommend the establishment of special clinics for the study and treatment of pain:[1]

> The pain clinic would allow the development of a battery of techniques to control pain. The pharmacological, sensory, and psychological methods of pain control do not exclude each other. A combination of several methods—such as electrical stimulation of nerves and appropriate drugs—may be necessary to provide satisfactory relief. The effective combination may differ for each type of pain and possibly for each individual depending on such factors as the patient's earlier medical history, pattern of spread of trigger zones, and the duration of pain; but it is only in a clinic, where many cases are seen and complete data files are kept, that sufficient experience and knowledge can be acquired to allow the best judgement in each case [p. 202].

Future directions

We can summarise some of the tasks of psychologists:

1   The manipulation of psychological variables to produce an effect on present pain experience or to prepare

an individual for predicted painful events. The physical recovery itself may also prove to be affected by psychological factors of the types discussed.

2 Development of more sophisticated methods for assessing subjective pain experiences, pain behaviour and complaints.

3 Investigation of pain from four points of view: pain thresholds, subjective experiences, pain complaints and pain behaviour (seeking help, self-medication, etc.) A case-history reported by Fordyce and his colleagues provides an interesting example of interdependence.[16] They described the treatment of a man who had complained of pain for many years, by changing the social consequences of his complaints of pain. Successful treatment of the complaint behaviour was followed by a marked decrease in pain behaviour (which had included withdrawal from daily activities, persistent resting and so on). Unfortunately they did not report his subjective estimates of the intensity of the pain, but one can infer that they must have decreased as the patient was able to return to normal activities after being incapacitated for eighteen years. When progress has been made along these lines it should be possible to gauge the effect of psychological factors on each aspect of the pain phenomena. It is also likely that a high rate of complaining sustains and even increases pain. There is almost certainly a high correlation between pain complaint and pain behaviour. It follows that reductions of any one of these four aspects of pain may lead to some reduction in the others. Naturally the interdependence and independence of these four components are matters of great interest for researchers and, we predict, will occupy the attention of psychologists for some considerable time.

4 Research into specific treatment techniques might

include the development of distraction routines, relaxation methods, testing the efficacy of suggestions, specific procedures to reduce anxiety about the outcome of an illness or operation, and so on. The biofeedback method (see Chapter 7) is a promising development which may help people to gain control of a specific biological subsystem. Its application in the treatment of certain types of headache is discussed in the next chapter.

5 Research into the relation between personality variables and the four major components of pain—thresholds, subjective experience, complaints and overt behaviour—offers intriguing possibilities.

4 A psychological approach to headaches

In the previous chapter a case was made for the introduction of psychological expertise into the study of pain. Headaches are a practical and common example to choose. The study of headaches is noteworthy for a profusion of psychological terms and concepts and for the absence of psychologists. It is to be hoped that the imminent arrival of psychologists will lead to the disappearance of the psychological claptrap that currently passes for explanation.

A valuable study of the prevalence of headaches in the community was carried out by Waters in a circumscribed area on a random sample of people selected from the electoral register.[1] Sixty-five per cent of the men and 79 per cent of the women in the sample reported that they had suffered from headaches in the previous year. In other surveys even higher figures were obtained.[2] Although it is not possible to establish exactly how costly a disorder headaches are in terms of suffering, money spent on medication or in working time lost, the figures are certain to be large. Some of the difficulties in obtaining precise estimates are the high rate of self-medication for headaches and the fact that headaches are seldom regarded as being sufficiently serious to require extended time off work and, hence, the absence of medical reports. However, it is possible to obtain some rough estimates of the extent of the problem by examining the expenditure on headache pills. In general practice in 1970, £0·7 million was attributed to consultations with general practitioners for migraine alone and prescription costs in the same year amounted to £1·6 million.[3] An American study published in 1968 estimated that 16 million people were taking $400 million worth of headache pills each year. So in terms of prevalence alone, headaches provide a challenge in the assessment of the potential contribution of psychologists to increasing our understanding of, and help in, modifying pain problems. If psychologists need other inducements to concern themselves with problems of headache, perhaps they will be provoked into action by the uncritical use of psychological concepts prevalent in the literature. For example, in a well-known text, muscular contraction headaches are attributed to 'psycho-sexual conflicts' and 'unresolved dependency needs.'[4] It is not merely that assertions of this kind are made in the absence of supporting evidence; there seems to be general agreement that psychological evidence is superfluous.

Less than half of the identified sufferers from headaches consult a medical practitioner for this complaint. What happens to those people who do seek treatment from a doctor? At present headaches are dealt with predominantly by general practitioners and neurologists. In daily practice, numbers of them appear to rely on a conception of pain that we have argued is now outdated. In both diagnosis and management, sensory input is held to be the most important factor, be it arterial constriction/dilation or muscular contraction, or both. Attempts at diagnosis and pharmacological intervention are directed towards the detection and reduction of this type of input to a central processing mechanism. In the case of detection, they try to establish the presence of physical changes by examining the symptoms (nausea, tenderness of the back of the neck and shoulders, etc.) produced by the postulated dysfunction or injury; in the case of reduction, the purpose is to restore the muscle or artery to normal functioning.

It would be wrong to assume, however, that there is no concern for psychological factors. Virtually all writers stress (perhaps incorrectly) that certain personality traits and attitudes are characteristic of headache sufferers. A Special Committee of neurologists and other physicians, convened in the United States in 1962 in an attempt to clarify the definitions of different types of headache, concluded that both physical and psychological factors contribute to the production of headaches. Indeed both types of factor are included in the formal definitions of headache.[5]

Many writers also emphasise the importance of psychological factors in the long-term amelioration of headaches. For example, Friedman in his discussion of migraine states that 'in the ability of the patient to handle emotional tension lies the most satisfactory means of preventing the attacks in the majority of cases' [p. 777].[6] In his discussion of muscular contraction headaches he invokes 'mental conflicts' as a key factor and recommends psychotherapy to relieve emotional tension and stress. In similar style, the author of a standard text on headaches says that the successful management of this problem requires no less than the 'amelioration and elimination of dissatisfaction and discontent' [p. 616].[4]

In most of the literature there is an imbalance between the assumptions on which diagnosis and treatment are based (especially the idea of blocking or reducing the input from the area of damage to the pain centre) and the acknowledged relevance of psychological factors to both etiology and treatment. The significance of psychological factors is often noted but seldom acted upon. In consequence, practitioners are left with little choice but to offer nebulous advice of the character quoted above, which is hardly useful. It can be argued, however, that this gap in the health services reflects more unfavourably on psychologists than on the medical profession.

Diagnosis and treatment

Before considering the contribution which psychologists can make, it is advisable briefly to review the prevailing practices and ideas on the subject. Ninety per cent of chronic sufferers from headache experience either muscular contraction headaches, vascular headaches of the migraine type or a combination of the two.[7] Of the total population of headache sufferers, only a tiny percentage suffer from injury or disease. In these cases the headache is associated with or results from cranial trauma, hypertension, tumor, etc. In an epidemiological study carried out by Waters, the prevalence of classical migraine was estimated to be 4 per cent in men and 7 per cent in women.[8] Data from other surveys make it likely that muscle-contraction headaches are three to four times more common than the migraine type. As we shall see, however, there are some difficulties in distinguishing satisfactorily between migraine, muscle tension and other types of headache.

Although many people refer to *any* recurrent severe headache as migraine, this loose usage is unhelpful. The Special Committee on headaches, referred to earlier, differentiated no less than fifteen different categories of headache.[5] However, for our purposes we can confine ourselves to the three most common of them. In classical migraine it is said that the onset of the headache is unilateral, preceded by visual prodromata (warn-

59

ings) and is accompanied by feelings of nausea and sometimes vomiting. It is said to be associated with a family history of similar headache, though Waters failed to confirm this. The quality of the pain is often described as being 'throbbing' as opposed to 'aching'.[4] It is also stressed that migraine often occurs during periods of relaxation—a feature which is said to distinguish it from the headaches attributed to muscle tension. It is widely believed that migraine results from vasoconstriction (narrowing of blood vessels) of certain intercranial arteries, followed by vasodilation (widening of the vessels) and distension, especially affecting the external carotid, the principal artery in the neck. Despite this view, for practical purposes diagnosis is generally based on the patient's subjective reports of his symptoms. Objective demonstration of vasoconstriction or dilation of vessels is rarely required and these changes have been monitored in surprisingly few studies. Different clinicians and writers on the subject tend to base their diagnoses on varying sets of the symptoms mentioned and to give them different degrees of importance. At present the three basic symptoms which appear to satisfy most authorities are: unilaterality, visual prodromata and nausea or vomiting. But when any one of these three is lacking and other factors are present it is left to the diagnostician to make his own judgement as to how the headache is to be classified. Presumably many of the doubtful cases might be clarified if greater use was made of physiological measurements of constriction, dilation and so on.

The second major type is muscular-contraction headache or, as it was previously called, 'psychogenic' headache. The diagnosis of this type of headache is not entirely satisfactory, despite the apparent simplicity of the definition offered by the Special Committee. 'Ache or sensation of tightness or pressure, or constriction, widely varied in intensity, frequency and duration . . . commonly sub-occipital. It is associated with sustained contraction of skeletal muscles in the absence of permanent structural change . . .'[5]

No measurement of the muscle tension associated with the locus of the symptom (on the head, neck or shoulders) is required for the diagnosis, although this is included as a diagnostic feature in the definition quoted. There is research evidence, however, that in these cases, muscle tension is in fact increased between and during headaches.[9] But our own research leads us to conclude that the connection between muscle tension and this type of headache is not always as direct or obvious as is generally supposed. It should also be borne in mind that in practice muscle-tension headaches tend to be identified by a process of exclusion. That is, they are headaches which are neither due to organic disease nor associated with classical migraine symptoms. They are headaches with bilateral onset, absence of nausea, no prodromata and little or no throbbing.

One of the major problems in attempting to arrive at discrete diagnoses is that many factors are common to the two major types of headache. This is not altogether surprising as it is more than likely that a severe attack of migraine may produce secondary muscular contractions, as a response to the pain. Similarly, severe attacks of muscle-contraction headache may result in secondary vasoconstriction of the relevant arteries. These mixed types of headache, comprising a combination of muscular and vascular symptoms, form the third major group. The sharp distinction drawn between vascular and muscular headaches appears to be convenient, if imprecise. It is possible that a continuum exists from mild to severe headaches in which the effect of the vascular changes becomes greater. It is to be hoped that psychologists may in time make a contribution to clarifying the similarities and distinctions between these different types of headaches.

There are many beliefs concerning the personality of headache sufferers that tend to be perpetuated by writers who depend almost entirely on clinical impression. The traditional beliefs about sufferers are that they are more intelligent, more neurotic, over-controlled, and so on. Claims about their distinctive personality are well illustrated in the following quotation from Friedman, which is characteristic of others.[10, 4] Friedman writes that: '[The migraine sufferer shows] adult perfectionism, rigidity, resentment, ambitiousness, efficiency, a constitutional predisposition to sustained emotional states' [p. 774].[6] And again a few pages later he writes of their 'inflexibility, over-conscientiousness, meticulousness, perfectionism, and resentment' [p. 776]. Martin and his colleagues summarised their view of the personality problems of muscle-contraction headache cases in this way: '. . . poorly repressed hostility is often evident, but unresolved dependency needs and psychosexual conflicts are also frequently present' [p. 203].[11]

It is also believed that migraine sufferers are not only more intelligent and predominantly from the professional classes, but that they have more visual defects, higher blood pressure and a strong family history of migraine. None of these claims were substantiated in the systematic investigations reported by Waters.[1, 8] He studied the association between the three main headache groups and the following characteristics: intelligence, social class, visual defects, level of blood pressure and family prevalence. When the results were compared with those obtained from appropriate control cases, *none* of the hypotheses were confirmed.

Few writers offer a description of sufferers from muscular-contraction headaches that is distinctly different; the demoralising lists of problems attributed to them rarely differ in length or content from those used in describing migraine sufferers. Despite the claims for the existence of clear diagnostic categories, the fact that the personality descriptions of tension-headache sufferers rarely differ from those ascribed to migraine cases reflects the uncritical reliance placed by non-psychological workers on psychoanalytic writings, from which no differential explanations about headache can be derived. Certainly, very few psychologists would have the courage to launch into generalisations about personality in the manner quoted here—for example, 'migraine sufferers are more rigid, ambitious, resentful', and so on. These lists of labels are rarely worth serious consideration. If all the personality labels applied to the headache patients were substantiated, they would be indistinguishable from a disturbed psychiatric population. When the necessary research is eventually carried out, few of the traditional beliefs about the relations between personality and headache are likely to survive. It should also be remembered that many of the difficulties apart from pain and discomfort reported by headache sufferers may as easily be a *response* to the experience of chronic pain and the consequent disruption of their life and responsibilities. *A priori* one can predict that a chronic complaint such as migraine will lead to resentment, irritability and even depression.

Most types of treatment are pharmacological, especially in cases of classical migraine. But in the light of current views on the role of psychological factors in the causation of migraine, it is usually thought desirable to provide psychotherapy to help the sufferer cope with his emotional conflicts. This recommendation is even more evident in discussions of the treatment for tension headaches. Despite these views on the need for psychotherapy, we have not located any studies in which the efficacy of psychotherapy for headache cases has been assessed. The dearth of evidence may be attributed in part to the fact that the recommended course of psychotherapy is rarely provided or accepted.

Some interesting results on the efficacy of pharmacological treatments have been reported. In several studies the most commonly recommended treatment for migraine, ergotamine, was found to be more effective than a placebo,[12] while in others no difference was detected.[1] Muscular relaxants, tranquillisers and analgesics are all used in the treatment of tension headaches but controlled trials are hard to find. However, it is commonly said that there are large individual differences in response to these drugs. An interesting point was made by Friedman who noted that, although the prescribed drugs reduced muscle tension, his patient continued to complain of tension headaches.[13] This finding can only increase doubts about the central role ascribed to muscle contractions in 'muscular-contraction headache', a definition which unfortunately incorporates a cause. Apart from the advice to undergo psychotherapy (which is seldom acted upon anyway) psychological treatments have so far played no serious part in the management of headaches.

Psychological research possibilities

The fact that psychologists have contributed little to the treatment of headaches is the clearest possible indication of the need for a period of research. Restricting ourselves mainly to those issues discussed in our brief review of the present state of headache control, we will try to sketch some of the opportunities for psychologists that are now beginning to emerge.

Although the mechanisms which precipitate the two main types of headache (migraine and tension headache) are generally agreed to be vascular and muscular respectively, objective measurements of these two types of function are rarely made when reaching diagnostic decisions. Psychophysiologists, with their specialised training in the recording and analysis of bodily functions of these types, have much to offer. In the case of

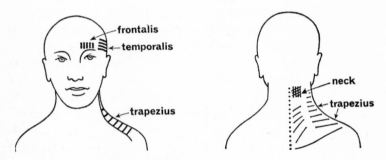

Diagram I   Head and neck muscles

tension headaches, they could record contractions of the muscles in the head and neck (trapezius, neck, frontalis, temporalis, etc.) during headache and headache-free episodes. Although they present some technical problems, recordings could also be made of the vasoconstriction and dilation of extra-cranial temporal arteries. Recordings of this character would enable psychologists to collaborate in the investigation of such problems as: (*a*) the hypothesised distinction between vascular, muscular and mixed headaches—to determine whether this division can be confirmed on the basis of objective measurements. Recordings carried out on the

c

mixed cases might also help to clarify which type of pharmacological (or other) treatment is most appropriate (for instance, a muscle relaxant); (*b*) the changes in key arteries and muscles between and during headaches, to see if there are signs of a return to normal between attacks or whether basal levels are persistently elevated. If the resting-levels are found to be high (and there is some evidence that this is so[14]) this might explain why in many cases headaches are said to occur after relatively minor stimulation.

Careful psychophysiological recording would also help to clarify the putative role of the frontalis muscle in tension headaches. This muscle, the most common locus of pain in this type of headache, may be a particularly difficult one to relax. Even when the patient is able to generally relax his body, it is not uncommon to find that the frontalis muscle is still partly contracted. For example, Balshan investigated the activity of sixteen different muscle groups and found that all but two of them showed highly correlated activity.[15] The exceptions were the frontalis and sternomastoid muscles. The resting-level of tension in the frontalis muscle was found to be far above that of the other fifteen muscles, during both rest and stimulation. This poor relationship between a generally relaxed state of the muscles and the continuing tension of the frontalis needs clarification; a search should also be undertaken for procedures that are capable of relaxing this resistant and important muscle.

For the most part doctors assess the quality of pain experiences on a rough subjective scale. This may consist of a five- or seven-point scale ranging from 'no headache' to 'mild', right up to 'incapacitatingly severe' headache. (The interesting step of relating these subjective reports of pain to objective psychophysiological changes has not yet been completed.) Although this sort of rough estimate has its uses, most obviously in daily practice, something more refined is needed for use when carrying out research into the quality of pain experiences. A new questionnaire developed by Melzack and Torgenson to assess twenty different qualities of pain experience, each along a dimension of intensity, may facilitate further studies of this type of question.[16] The respondent has to indicate which adjectives in the list provided best describe his pain, for example flickering, beating, quivering, throbbing, pounding, pulsing, etc. We can illustrate the possibilities of this psychological approach with an example. Although there is a strong belief that vascular headaches are 'throbbing' while muscular ones are 'aching', no adequate study has been performed in which the intensity of the pain experienced is used as a covariant. In other words, it may be that as a headache increases in intensity it is more likely to be described as throbbing. Research using a scale of the type developed by Melzack, with separate dimensions for quality and intensity, permits analysis of this type of question.

Although psychologists' contributions to treatment have so far been confined to explorations with the techniques of relaxation and of biofeedback (see Chapter 7) they are in a strong position to contribute methodologically to the design of controlled trials to assess the efficacy of psychotherapeutic and pharmacological treatments. In seeking a comprehensive view of treatment effects it might be desirable to measure physiological changes (e.g. frontalis tension), pain complaints (quality and intensity as well as duration and frequency) and pain behaviour itself. If research on the not dissimilar subject of fear is any guide,[17] it will be found that although these three variables are well correlated, they show a degree of independent variation. It is probable that a certain amount of de-synchrony will be found, with the three measures changing at different speeds. Awareness of this possibility is of practical as well as theoretical interest, in that therapeutic conclusions drawn from the changes observed in one of the three variables may give a misleading picture. The possibility of de-synchrony relates to a suggestion made in the previous chapter, that psychological factors may play a more significant role in less severe pain. Consequently, as intense pains diminish the deliberate manipulation of attention, suggestion and other psychological factors should expedite further improvements. Once one has determined the level at which psychological factors can be successfully manipulated, it becomes possible to reduce drug dosages and finally withdraw them.

It is possible to see several strategies which psychologists might employ in their approach to the problems of pain control. In the first place they could attempt to reduce basic background levels of tension by means of techniques such as relaxation training. A second possibility is the use of specific self-control procedures to control key muscles or vascular functions (see Chapter 7). A third possibility is the development of various techniques for coping with trigger stimuli that are known to precipitate headaches. For example, social anxiety and neurotic fears are said to produce headaches when people with these types of vulnerability are placed in social situations. If this is confirmed, treatment techniques such as desensitisation or flooding (see Chapter 9, pp. 144–146) should prove to be therapeutically useful. It is also worth mentioning the importance of the reactions of other people in sustaining the complaints of chronic headache sufferers. Research on other types of complaint behaviour has shown that the frequency of this behaviour is determined in part by the manner in which other people respond to it. Intense and regular interest shown in the sufferer's complaints will probably increase the frequency of complaining, whereas comparative indifference is likely to be followed by a decline in the frequency of complaining. Modification of the patient's expectation of the attention which follows excessive complaining entails giving advice not only to the patient himself but also to the people who have a main part in his life. It was observed in the case-study mentioned on p. 54 of the previous chapter[18] that disregard for the headache complaints of a chronic sufferer, combined with increased attention and social rewards for healthy activities unrelated to his preoccupation with headaches, greatly reduced the amount of the complaints.

Although it is easy to elaborate further plans for psychological research in headaches, we have no desire to compose lists of unrealistic schemes. Our principal aim is to show how psychologists and physicians can combine their interests and expertise in opening new avenues.

5 Sleep disorders

Disorders of sleep are extremely common. The most frequent complaints are of insomnia—difficulty in falling asleep or in staying asleep. It has been estimated in surveys that from one-sixth to one-quarter of the adult population in Britain is affected by sleep problems,[1,2] and in psychiatric conditions this proportion rises to 45 per cent. In addition to insomnia, there are sleep disorders which affect only a small number of people. These include such problems as somnambulism (sleep-walking), head-banging (jactatio capitis nocturna), nocturnal bed-wetting (enuresis), night terrors and nightmares.

Intense research over the past two decades has increased our knowledge about sleep, but many problems remain. We are still unclear about the function of sleep or how much of it we need in order to feel refreshed, satisfied and capable of normal functioning. Expansion of physiological knowledge has outstripped psychological understanding and this uneven development helps to account for the narrowness of prevailing approaches to treatment.

As doctors generally prescribe sleeping tablets (hypnotics) for insomnia, there is a large consumption of these drugs. In 1964 for example, 10 per cent of National Health prescriptions in England and Wales were for hypnotic drugs, and in the United States the sales of these drugs and tranquillisers rose by 535 per cent between 1952 and 1967.

Dunlop has estimated that in Britain one night's sleep in ten is induced by hypnotic drugs.[3] Or to put it another way, using his estimate as a basis, we can say that on any night $3\frac{1}{2}$ million people in England and Wales will take sleeping pills. Despite its evident popularity, we hope to show why an exclusively pharmacological approach to treatment is not satisfactory.

As we have said, research into sleep has been predominantly physiological and pharmacological, with a sprinkling of psychological studies. Regrettably little work has been carried out on the psychological question of central importance—sleep satisfaction. It is undoubtedly as important to know how much sleep is required for psychological as for physical restoration. At present we have little reason for supposing that the two types of needs, physical and psychological, are always fulfilled simultaneously. Nor do we know whether both needs are met by the same amount or the same type of sleep. It seems likely that individual differences in psychological need will be greater than the differences in physical need, given comparable physical exertions, stature and so on. As many people who complain of sleeplessness do not in fact sleep for shorter periods than do good sleepers, it is important to determine the factors that affect a person's judgement of how long, and how well, he sleeps. Considerations of this type lead naturally to questions of how psychologists can best contribute to the understanding and modification of sleep disorders. But before examining the possibilities, it is necessary to give a short account of the nature of sleep.

The nature of sleep

A strong daily pattern of sleeping and waking develops with age. Babies gradually adopt a pattern of sleeping

71

at night and being awake during the day; at one year old they have two phases of sleep (night and afternoon nap) and by five years old they usually follow the pattern of their parents. Babies average about 16·6 hours of sleep a day, but as they grow and mature children require less sleep. By the ages of thirty to forty most people average about 7·4 hours of sleep each day, and this amount declines slowly until at the age of seventy, one may sleep as little as 6 hours in twenty-four. Taking the adult population as a whole, the average nightly sleep is roughly 7·5 hours. It is important to remember, however, that there are large individual differences at all ages but particularly in the very young and the very old. There is also a small number of adults who appear to be adequately refreshed after as little as three to four hours of sleep. For most people this small ration would amount to insomnia, but for the lucky small percentage it appears to produce no problems and has been called 'healthy insomnia'.[4]

Contrary to earlier beliefs, sleep is not a period of mental and physical inactivity. It is an active process during which incessant but so far poorly understood mental activity continues, though in a different form from that which occurs during waking hours. Originally, the depth of sleep was estimated by ascertaining the amount of external stimulation necessary to awaken a sleeper. However, in recent years this has been supplemented, and almost replaced, by measures of the electrical activity of the brain (EEG), popularly known as brain-waves.

When a person is awake and alert but with his eyes closed, brain-waves of 8–13 cycles per second (the alpha rhythm) can be recorded from the back of his head.[5] With the onset of drowsiness these alpha rhythms gradually decrease, and the person reports a drifting or floating of consciousness. The onset of sleep is commonly defined as the point at which these rhythms disappear; consciousness is lost and responses to external stimuli are greatly diminished. Sleep can be divided into two major classes: rapid eye movement sleep (REM or paradoxical) and non-rapid eye movement sleep (non-REM or orthodox sleep). REM sleep, as the name suggests, is characterised by frequent bursts of rapid jerky eye movements and these are accompanied by very slow brain-waves (2–6 cycles per second) of a low voltage. In non-REM sleep there are very few rapid eye movements, and although the brain-waves continue at a slow rate, they are of high voltage and faster frequency (12–14 cycles per second). Most research workers subdivide non-REM sleep into a further four stages on the basis of small differences in brain-wave patterns, but for our purposes these details of sleep stages are not pertinent. Further information is available in the texts by Kleitman[6] and Oswald.[5]

In the early stages of research into this new classification of sleep, dreaming was believed to occur only when the eyes moved rapidly (REM sleep). It is certainly true that about 75 per cent of people awakened from REM sleep have been dreaming, in contrast to only about 7 per cent of those in orthodox sleep. However, it now seems probable that REM periods are associated more with dreaming in the sense of fantasy occurrences, while non-REM periods are associated with 'thinking' of recent events or experiences. Although we can recall precious little of it, it appears that we dream for at least two out of the average seven and a half hours we sleep each night. During the rest of the sleep period we probably 'think' a great deal.

Sleep deprivation

Experience of depriving individuals of all or part of their sleep has revealed how essential sleep is for normal functioning; it has also shown the relative importance of certain types or stages of sleep. It is sometimes claimed that after prolonged deprivation of sleep people become acutely disturbed and exhibit bizarre behaviour. Certainly some extraordinary cases have been reported, but the appearance of extremely disturbed behaviour depends on many factors including the individual's mental stability, physical condition and expectations. On the whole it is true that unstable or disturbed people are more susceptible to the adverse effects of sleep deprivation. For most people the behavioural changes seen after deprivation are predictable and apart from fatigue include irritability, inability to concentrate and periods of disorientation and misperception. Lapses occur in the performance of tasks, particularly when the person is required to respond quickly. Although complete restoration of function takes a few days, we are fortunate in having the capacity for quick recovery. Even after going without sleep for as long as 200 hours, dramatic reversals can occur after a single long sleep (twelve to fourteen hours). Williams found a 90 per cent recovery of efficiency after one such sleep,[7] but in his particularly careful research Wilkinson detected the persistence of subtle difficulties.[8]

During 'recovery sleep' a rebound phenomenon is consistently observed. It appears that after deprivation there is a need for certain types of sleep. This is inferred from the fact that the percentage of time spent in particular stages of sleep shows a marked increment for a short period before it returns to the sleeper's usual level. The rebound effect is strongest after loss of **REM** sleep, which is the first to be 'repaid' after a period of total sleep deprivation. If, instead of total restriction of sleep, one merely prevents one type of sleep, the same rebound phenomenon is seen to occur even within the period of sleep itself.

Sleeping tablets

The effects of sleep-inducing drugs have been fully investigated by EEG analyses. The sleep patterns of drug users have been documented and the effects of drug withdrawal on their brain-wave patterns have also been studied. Because of the widespread prescription of hypnotic drugs to people complaining of sleep difficulties, it is worth reviewing the main findings. Kales notes that 'most physicians are unfamiliar with the basic sleep and dream cycles and the changes induced in them by hypnotic agents. Therefore they do not often ask patients how they sleep after sleeping pills have been prescribed or withdrawn.'[9] In fact, virtually all the hypnotics produce similar disturbances of sleep pattern. Characteristically, there is a suppression of REM activity and of sleep stages 3 and 4, coupled with a marked delay in the occurrence of the first REM period. Upon withdrawal of the drug, especially after chronic use, there is a rebound effect in which the first REM period occurs early in the night and the total REM time increases. Disturbances can also occur during this period and include nightmares, insomnia and dissatisfaction with the quality of sleep. Unfortunately psychologists have so far shown little interest in the question of psychological restoration following the use of hypnotic drugs. It is true that after taking these drugs the person will probably fall asleep more quickly and sleep for a longer period. However, as there will be no REM sleep,

75

there may be adverse psychological consequences of this deprivation despite the fact that the person is sleeping through the night.

A large proportion of people suffering from insomnia have psychiatric disorders—depression, anxiety neuroses and so on. As many of these patients already experience less REM sleep (they do not merely sleep for a shorter time), treatment with hypnotic drugs may inadvertently aggravate some aspects of their sleep problems. It is in fact possible that some of the symptoms are exacerbated by a loss of REM sleep. As Hawkins puts it, 'Hypnotic drugs do not have any substantive value for chronic insomnia and may in fact compound the problem due to the additional disruptions in pattern.'[10] The rebound effects experienced after withdrawal of sleeping pills may contribute to the development of a dependence on these drugs, particularly if the doctor fails to prepare his patient for after-effects, the most notable of which are nightmares. Gradual withdrawal, with supportive explanations of the expected drug-induced physiological alterations in sleep pattern and their psychological consequences, may well be of importance. A careful psychological study of the role of doctors in preventing dependence on sleeping pills is overdue.

We need a psychology of sleep to complement the physiology of sleep. In particular we require far more psychological information about the subjective reports which people give of their sleep experiences and satisfactions (and how to relate these to psychological assessments of sleep durations and patterns). For example, Hauri reports that when people have slept well they are less moody, better able to concentrate and less tired physically.[11] This is consistent with findings that a cheerful mood increases as the length of sleep time increases from five to nine hours. However, it has been observed that the sleeper's mood deteriorates when he sleeps for more than nine hours at a stretch. When it is not needed, excessive amounts of sleep seem to lead to discomfort and people complain of feeling 'worn out'. Subjective estimates of poor sleep, on the other hand, have been related to several factors; reduced total sleep time, longer time taken to fall asleep, less stage 4 sleep and less REM sleep. As we have already seen, poor sleep is associated with deteriorations in mood and concentration and with increased irritability.

Insomnia

At present, the therapeutic approach to insomnia is mainly pharmacological. A psychological approach has the merit of freshness and may help to clarify some of the persistent problems. Insomnia refers either to difficulties in falling asleep or in staying asleep, or both, but subjective estimates of how long we take to fall asleep or how long we have remained asleep do not correspond closely to the facts. For example, Schwartz studied a group of patients who complained that they scarcely slept during the night. Using EEG criteria, he found that they slept throughout the greater part of the night but woke frequently for brief periods. On the following morning they claimed that they had not slept at all; their perception of the amount of sleep was grossly distorted.[12] Another common misperception of poor sleepers was described by Munro.[13] His subjects were classified as either good or poor sleepers on the basis of the same EEG criteria. Good sleepers estimated that it took them about seven minutes to fall asleep and this was subsequently confirmed in the sleep laboratory. Poor sleepers, on the other hand, estimated that it took them just short of one hour to fall asleep. In fact it was found that they took a mere eight minutes longer than the good sleepers. However, the poor sleepers did not overestimate on every aspect of sleep and were reasonably accurate in estimating the number of times they awoke during the night. Misperceptions of the time of falling asleep and the duration of sleep are important because hypnotic drugs are prescribed in response to complaints made by patients—and in reaching their decisions about prescribing these drugs, doctors have to rely on their patient's own account of his sleep satisfaction.

It is possible that the misperceptions are caused in part by the heightened physiological arousal observed in poor sleepers both before sleep and early in the sleeping period. They commonly experience accelerations of heart rate, increased vaso-constriction and higher rectal temperature. Findings of this type encourage the hope that action taken before going to sleep (such as relaxation) may help people to fall asleep more easily and to benefit more from it. We already have some evidence that relaxation can be put to good therapeutic use in helping students to overcome mild insomnia (see p. 81).

The fact that at least two types of misperception concerning the extent of sleeplessness have been identified does not mean that sufferers are faking their sleep problems. Rather, it emphasises the heterogeneity of the group of people who complain about sleeplessness. They range from people who sleep an average number of hours but underestimate the time they spend asleep or who do not feel refreshed afterwards, to those who both claim and manifest a chronic shortage of sleep. People with psychiatric complaints and the old fall mainly into this latter group.

What factors determine a person's judgement of the

adequacy of his sleep? There are the obvious ones, such as feelings of physical fatigue, discomfort in the eyes and painful muscles on awakening. Another important element is his assessment of how efficiently he works. Wilkinson has analysed the ways in which performance can be impaired by varying amounts of sleep deprivation and his findings include evidence of lapses in performance, marked by voluntary and involuntary pauses in activity.[7] This deterioration apparently can be reduced if the person is allowed to pace a task for himself, if the length of the task is shortened, or if he can be highly motivated.

An interesting determinant of sleep satisfaction, which is as obvious as it is neglected, arises from each person's beliefs about his sleep needs. We develop a conception of how much sleep we need on the basis of past experience, and our judgement of the benefit derived from any single night's sleep is made on this basis. Such evaluations of sleep are to some extent idiosyncratic. It remains to be seen whether these personal conceptions are open to modification and, if so, what effects successful modification would have on sleeping habits and the benefit derived from sleep. These and the related psychological questions are both intrinsically interesting and potentially useful.

Anxiety has been shown to affect both the speed of the onset of sleep and the number of awakenings during the night; these are two crucial factors in sleeplessness. There is also some indirect evidence that the reduction of anxiety facilitates improved sleep, and as we hope to show in Chapter 9, the alleviation of anxiety is the psychologist's strong hand. When psychologists turn their attention to sleep disorders we can expect them to explore the clinical value of their anxiety-reduction methods as an early priority. It is worth bearing in mind that other states or activities which produce heightened arousal, such as concentrated study or intense physical exercise, also retard the onset of sleep. In the hands of informative general practitioners these facts can be put to clinical use simply and effectively. So, patients complaining of insomnia might be reminded to avoid drinking coffee in the evening, taught to use relaxation exercises before going to bed, and advised not to engage in intense physical or mental activities within an hour or two before retiring.

It has been claimed that stress reduces the amount of time spent in the deepest stage of sleep, which is the stage closely associated with mental and physical refreshment. This may help to explain the reported sense of fatigue following sleep taken during periods of stress. There are also data which indicate that sleep requirements change during times of stress or increased mental or physical work. At these times more sleep is needed in order to achieve comparable refreshment.

To summarise, the psychological state of the person just before sleep can lead to disturbances of the onset, continuity and duration of sleep. And it is these characteristics that affect the sleeper's estimate of sleep satisfaction. Consequently, improved control of anxiety and avoidance of intense physical or intellectual activities just before sleep can contribute to sleep satisfaction. Modification of patients' conceptions of their sleep needs may also be of some therapeutic value.

Psychological treatments

We shall not discuss pharmacological approaches to treatment as they have already been briefly considered. The need for other approaches arises from the problems associated with hypnotic drugs, such as dependence and rebound effects, especially when they are used over long periods. These drugs seem to be most effective when immediate results are needed, as in acute, circumscribed crises rather than in chronic disorders. For less severe problems non-pharmacological means are to be preferred. In these cases, placebos, relaxation or repeated monotonous stimulation may suffice. Variants of relaxation, systematic desensitisation and hypnotic relaxation have been used, sometimes to good effect. For example, Borkovec and Fowles achieved some success in helping female college students with their sleeping difficulties.[14] Forty girls were allotted to one of four groups: self-relaxation, therapist-administered relaxation, hypnotic relaxation or a control group who were not treated. Each of the treated girls received three therapy sessions each lasting one hour, and instructions to practise the relaxation techniques just before going to bed. All three of the treated groups reported significant improvement after therapy, while the girls who had no treatment showed no change. In a second study, by Steinmark and Borkovec, forty-eight students with sleep problems were randomly assigned to relaxation treatment, relaxation and desensitisation to the state of sleep itself, placebo or a no-treatment control. In a carefully conducted experiment they were able to conclude that all three treated groups showed significantly greater improvement than the untreated students. Relaxation therapy, with or without desensitisation, proved to be particularly useful.[15] Further developments along these lines are anticipated. It is to be hoped that the findings will be confirmed and extended; it would be advisable to include objective assessments of sleep loss and sleep changes in addition to the sleepers' own reports of sleep onset and satisfaction. In cases of severe insomnia it may be necessary to combine psychological methods of

81

treatment with tranquillising drugs or even with hypnotics.

Psychologists can also help people who are concerned that they are getting too little sleep and who are over-estimating the amount of sleep they are losing. It would be of interest, for example, to see how far judgements of sleep satisfaction can be modified by giving the person information—both true and false—concerning the actual length of sleep. With appropriate technical assistance, it may also be possible for people to induce sleep, defined here as the disappearance of alpha rhythms, by feedback techniques (see Chapter 7) in which they are taught to reduce the occurrence of their alpha rhythms. Although this technique has been successfully demonstrated in the laboratory, it has not so far been used to induce sleep. Psychologists may also be able to help in dealing with the problem of drug dependence by arranging graded and supported reductions in dosage of drugs. As an easy start, clearer information can be provided to the users of hypnotics in order to anticipate and perhaps reduce the psychological upsets experienced after withdrawal of the tablets. Placebos may also be of use in this respect when dealing with mild cases of insomnia.

Case illustrations

Two cases of successful psychological modification will help to give some idea of the opportunities available. Repetitive stimulation by auditory tones was used with a fair amount of success in one of our patients. She was a young nurse who had become addicted to barbiturates in her attempts to sleep during the day when she was on night shifts. Without barbiturates she had been unable to sleep and therefore unable to work efficiently the next night. It led to her stealing drugs while on duty and her career was in jeopardy. Following drug withdrawal, she slept, on an average, two to three hours a night, with a very late sleep onset following many anxious hours of trying to fall asleep. A treatment was developed to lower her general state of high arousal and to speed the onset of sleep. At first she was to entertain herself in pleasant but not highly stimulating tasks until about 2 A.M. Then she was to go to bed, practise her relaxation exercises and listen to a tape of auditory signals of low intensity that were repeated every few seconds. The tape was designed to be monotonous and thereby reduce central vigilance. The patient began to fall asleep more quickly and for longer periods. With this improvement, she began her night progressively earlier. She worked back until she was sleeping six to seven hours a night from about 11 P.M. Although one might have expected a gradual recovery from the addicted state with time, it was felt that the treatment had substantially increased the rate of recovery and led to the patient sleeping even longer than she had before the night-shift disturbance.

Another patient treated by one of the authors showed an interesting relationship between her phobia and a persistent nightmare. The patient was referred for treatment of a phobia of worms and snakes which had led to her becoming virtually housebound. During the initial interview, she also complained of a disturbed sleep pattern. She frequently dreamt that she was standing on the edge of an open grave and this repeated nightmare had disturbed her for many years.

A psychological treatment known as flooding (see Chapter 9) was successfully used to reduce the phobic reaction to worms. The patient was enabled once again to go out and about without any fears, pick up and hold worms, and so on. Towards the end of the short treatment for the phobia she reported sleeping much better and that she had stopped dreaming of graves and coffins. Although no precise explanation could be found for the relation between the phobia and her nightmares, it is of interest that the elimination of the fear was followed by the disappearance of the nightmare. It seems possible that her considerable anxiety during the day may have persisted during sleep periods, thereby making nightmares more likely. The reduction of her anxiety was therefore followed by undisturbed sleep.

Nocturnal bed-wetting

Studies of the prevalence of bed-wetting (enuresis) in Britain and elsewhere uniformly show that this habit declines with age. Between 10 per cent and 20 per cent of children are still wetting at four and half years of age, but this proportion declines roughly to 5 per cent by the age of 9 and only 2 per cent by the age of fifteen.[16] At all ages, slightly more boys than girls are bed-wetters.

For a long time it was erroneously believed that bed-wetting is a symptom of generalised emotional or psychiatric disorder. As numerous psychological investigations[17, 18, 19, 20, 21] have failed to find any significant relationship between bed-wetting and maladjustment, speculations about the underlying meaning of enuresis need to be scrutinised with care. Excluding those uncommon cases in which a physical dysfunction is responsible or where there is severe psychological disturbance, bed-wetting in childhood is best regarded as simply a developmental disorder. It is, incidentally, a disorder that tends to run in families. Young and Turner have estimated that in the cases of between 60 per cent and 70 per cent of children suffering from enuresis who come for professional assistance there are, or have been, other sufferers in their families.[21]

If bed-wetting is not seen as a symptom of emotional disorder, psychotherapeutic treatment is unlikely to be appropriate. Contrary to the belief held by many people engaged in Child Guidance work, psychotherapy does not reduce bed-wetting. In two investigations of this possibility bed-wetters who received psychotherapy did no better than those who received no treatment at all.[22, 23] It needs to be borne in mind that it is a developmental disorder; most bed-wetters will achieve continence, in time, without treatment.

It follows that the usual purpose of treatment is to expedite the natural but sometimes unacceptably slow development of continence. So far, psychological treatment has proved the most successful method of achieving this end. The bell-and-pad alarm method of conditioning treatment, in which a bell wakens the child as soon as he wets the sheets, helps to achieve continence in roughly six to eight weeks, in approximately 70 per cent of cases.[24, 25, 26, 27] The oustanding problems with this type of treatment include the need to reduce the unacceptably large relapse rate, to improve parental cooperation and to clarify the theoretical basis of the treatment.

Nightmares

Nightmares vary from unpleasant dreams to intense night-terrors, and can be related to factors like alcohol addiction, withdrawal from drugs and periods of past or present stress. But this is not always so. Some people suffer from periodic or repeated nightmares for no detectable reason. Fisher and his colleagues identified three types of nightmare by relating them to the EEG activity present at the onset of the nightmare. The most intense and pathological nightmares occur not during REM periods but in stage 4, deep sleep. They start without warning and are associated with sudden, intense activity of the autonomic nervous system, including increased heart rate and respiratory rate. The sleeper does not react to external stimuli, cannot be wakened, appears mentally confused and disoriented and is unable to recall the dream. Fisher gives this description of a typical sufferer. His nightmare began with a 'sudden loud scream of blood-curdling intensity'. About six out of ten of his nightmares, these outbreaks of uncontrolled anxiety, took place during the first period of non-REM sleep, after one and a half hours of sleep. The subject passed instantly into a highly aroused state 'in which he appeared to be dis-associated, confused, unresponsive to his environment and hallucinating. His heart rate increased within 30 seconds from 64 beats per minute to 152 beats per minute.' Afterwards he could recall next to nothing of the nightmare.[28]

The second type of nightmare usually occurs during REM sleep and often is associated with anxiety dreams. In these cases, the anxiety is preceded by a more gradual increase in cardiac and respiratory activity. In absolute terms the increase is smaller (heart rate increases of between fifteen and twenty beats per minute), but is nevertheless associated with subjective sensations of racing heart and other feelings of anxiety. On awakening this heightened physiological state reverts quickly to normal. Generally the person can recall the dream afterwards.

Finally there are nightmares that awaken sleepers from stage 2 sleep. These are not heralded by cardiovascular changes but do show moderate increases in heart rate following awakening (they are not nearly as intense as stage 4 nightmares).

Little has been contributed from a psychological point of view to the reduction of nightmares of any variety. It seems likely that the last two types mentioned, REM and stage 2 dreams, can be influenced by day-time manipulations as well as by night-time interferences. Successful attempts to modify daily anxiety or stress may of course reduce the frequency or intensity of the nightmares.

In the case of recurring dreams, the formation of relevant habits might de-fuse the disturbing thoughts both in the day and the night. Having acknowledged that sleeping is an active process during which the mind is occupied, though in an unusual way, it would be interesting to investigate how much control a person can acquire over his 'thinking' while dreaming. Is it possible to achieve a degree of self-control over the content of one's dreams by conscious focusing and switching of one's thoughts, in preparation, as it were, for the night's dream-work?

Night-time 'interference' refers to attempts to control nightmares by autonomic monitoring. When signs of a disturbing dream sequence begin to emerge on autonomic tracings, external stimulation could be introduced to lighten the sleep. It is hoped that this will result in an avoidance of the nightmare. The fearful stage 4 nightmares, which come without warning, could not be dealt with in this way, and, in any event, excessive interference with stage 4 sleep might produce problems of its own, arising out of the consequent deprivation of this type of sleep.

In concluding, we hope that the facts and notions set out here will encourage psychologists and doctors to enlarge their view of sleep problems by incorporating neglected but important psychological factors. The opportunities for expanding our comprehension of ordinary and disturbed sleep are excellent and in time will no doubt improve the range and quality of clinical help available to insomniacs and other sufferers.

6 Placebo power

The prescription of pills plays a major part in contemporary medicine. To the millions of drugs prescribed by doctors each year, we must add twice as many which are taken without prescription. We also know that crucial elements in determining and maintaining the epidemic of pill-taking are psychological: many of the effects produced by the pills are wholly psychological, others partly so. Even if psychologists restricted themselves solely to understanding the psychology of pill-taking, their active participation in medical specialities additional to psychiatry would be fully justified.

It has been observed that medicine-taking is a common activity, frequently indulged in, often over long periods. It serves a variety of needs, many of them social and psychological rather than purely pharmacological.[1] Extensive research has established beyond any doubt that swallowing substances of no medicinal value in the form of a pill (placebo) is capable of producing powerful psychological effects. This single fact plays a valuable part in attempts to explain the astonishing incidence of pill-taking and the ever-increasing variety of tablets, both prescribed and not-prescribed, available on the market. It also helps to explain why patients expect very commonly to be given pills when they pay a visit to the doctor—and in turn, it helps to account for the way in which this expectation has influenced doctors so that they prescribe pills readily and frequently. Before embarking on an examination of

some of the major psychological factors which contribute to the power of placebos, it is as well to provide
some facts and opinions about the pill-taking habits of
patients—and the prescribing habits of doctors.

In 1967 the health authorities in Hartlepool invited
people to return their unused medicines, and they received no less than 43,000 tablets within one week—
from only 500 homes. This is nearly ninety tablets per
home. As part of the same investigation, a survey carried
out in homes in the same area revealed that 94 per cent
of them contained some non-prescribed medicine and 29
per cent of all the medicines found had been in the
house for longer than a year. They also estimated that
roughly 6 per cent of the prescribed medicines which
patients have actually gone to the trouble of having
made up are not used. In Britain, it has been estimated
that the cost of vitamin tablets to the National Health
Service amounts to several million pounds each year, and
this of course does not take account of the considerably
greater sums spent on purchasing proprietary preparations from pharmacies and other shops. Commenting on
these habits, Dunlop points out that while vitamin
supplements are desirable in the diet of pregnant
women, infants and some old people, 'there is no scientific evidence that in healthy people vitamins prevent infections, stimulate appetite, help to assuage neuritic
pains or aid positive health in any way'. He concludes
that 'the wholesale consumption of vitamin concentrates
... is a waste of money'.[2]

As we stated earlier, Dunlop reckons that in Britain
roughly one person in every ten takes a hypnotic drug,
such as a barbiturate, to be able to sleep. It seems that
'people want to turn consciousness on and off like a tap'.

One has to consider also the consequences of extensive over-prescribing in producing the adverse side

effects which accompany many of the most effective drugs. Wade quotes evidence to show that the more drugs a person receives, the more likely he is to suffer adverse reactions.[3] In one study the proportion of adverse reactions observed in patients receiving between one and five drugs was 18 per cent but rocketed to over 80 per cent in patients receiving more than five drugs simultaneously. Despite the increased risks involved and our ignorance about the synergistic effects of taking several drugs at the same time, multiple prescribing has become a common practice. In an example quoted by Dunlop, patients in a reputable American hospital were found to be receiving, *on average*, no less than fourteen drugs at the same time (small wonder that nurses have so little time to talk to their patients). None of the patients investigated in this survey had had less than six types of drug and one of them had received as many as thirty-two. Unwittingly perhaps, many patients have taken avoidance action. As we saw earlier, many prescriptions are not made up and we also know that few people seem to take the tablets 'as prescribed'. An example of the way in which patients in a surgical ward disposed of drugs was described in Chapter 2. None of the eight pseudo-patients who simulated insanity in the study reported by Rosenhan (described on page 161) were regarded as uncooperative.[4] Nevertheless they managed to collect and store all the 2,000 tablets they were given in hospital.

The other drug problem

Figures describing national drug-taking habits are so astronomic as to border on the meaningless. Dunlop, for example, has calculated that in the first twenty years of the operation of the National Health Service in

Britain the drug bill increased more than fivefold.[2] Again, the number of Health Service prescriptions rose from 206 million in 1963 to 256 million in 1972, at a cost of £211 million. In their survey of pill-taking habits, Dunnett and Cartwright found that no less than 55 per cent of their respondents had taken some form of medicine in the preceding twenty-four hours; two-thirds of all these medicines were not prescribed. Perhaps even more striking is the fact that 40 per cent of the adults had taken some form of medicine *on each day* of the two-week period prior to the enquiry. As they point out, taking medicine is 'not only a common but also a frequent activity for many people'. According to the authors, most of the pills were palliative and 'probably a great deal would be illogical or irrelevant in simple pharmacological terms . . . but the efficacy of medicine does not depend only on its pharmacological properties'.

It is hard to tell whether the widespread prescription of drugs by doctors is a response to public demand or vice versa. Although it is true that in the Dunnett and Cartwright survey it emerged that two-thirds of all the medicines the respondents had taken were non-prescribed, this should be seen against the background of a patient's expectation from a consultation with his doctor—for the same authors found that in two-thirds of the medical consultations they studied, the doctor concluded by writing a prescription. They also learnt that many doctors feel they would prescribe less if they had more time to spend with their patients. In any event, it seems that whether one attends a doctor or stays at home, the pharmaceutical industry benefits.

When does a person with a complaint stay at home and when does he attend his doctor's consulting-room? From this survey, it is clear that people seek medical advice for only a small proportion of their complaints, probably less than a third of them. It was found that although 92 per cent of the adults had some symptom in a two-week period, only 16 per cent had consulted their doctor. Instead, they seek advice elsewhere (commonly from a chemist) or treat themselves by medication or other means. The most common medicine taken by the respondents in the sample under description consisted of pain-killers. Forty-one per cent of those interviewed had taken at least one such pill in the preceding two weeks. The other popular medicines were laxatives and skin ointments. The evidence seems to suggest that self-medication is the most common alternative to visiting the doctor. There are however important differences of opinion both among patients and in the medical profession themselves about which problems or complaints justify a visit to the doctor. Some doctors believe that the public should be encouraged to treat themselves as much as possible, while others hold the conservative view that patients should seek medical advice about most of their complaints.

It should not be thought that all the evidence obtained in this investigation was discouraging. Among other findings it turned out that the majority of patients do accept their doctors' advice about what medicine to take, do get their prescriptions made up and do use at least some of them. Some common reasons for the incorrect use of drugs—usually a failure to continue taking them for the period prescribed—include improvement of symptoms, fears of addiction and negative attitudes towards drug-taking. Another encouraging finding to emerge from this and other studies is the declining passion for laxatives. There has in fact been a dramatic drop in the previously widespread, unwarranted and almost daily use of laxatives.

In his passing mention of this problem, Dunlop remarks that in the earlier view of digestive troubles the colon 'was regarded as a poisonous cesspit', but now 'it is more generally realised that moderate constipation constitutes a far smaller menace to health than over-enthusiastic efforts to treat it'.

The decline in the use of laxatives reflects a change in attitudes towards digestive processes that can be regarded as a triumph of medical education. For anyone who feels that we exaggerate, here are some selections from a well-known, popular book of medical advice published in the 1920s by Dr Robert Bell, when he was Vice-President of the International Society for Cancer Research. He was a prominent physician of his time. The quotations are taken from the fifth edition of *Woman in Health and Sickness* (1923).[5] Care of the digestive processes is given a central place in hygiene.

> Constipation is probably the most frequent source of trouble that the female has to contend with. It generally originates in carelessness and want of attention to the daily evacuation of the bowels. Mothers cannot be too particular in insisting upon their children paying a daily visit to the WC.

This advice must be adhered to because 'many of the illnesses which young girls are liable to are the direct effect of neglect of this simple hygienic precaution'. We cannot quote all the ills and misfortunes awaiting those foolish girls who fail to take Dr Bell's advice, but note that 'some people have recourse to an aperient whenever a headache manifests itself, and as a rule they are right, because the bowels are usually at fault'. Hysteria calls for a battery of remedies and 'the bowels should also be carefully regulated and pills taken regularly for two weeks'. Displacement of the womb? The womb should be retained by the use of 'suitable mechanical appliances' and general treatment requires that 'the bowels should be carefully regulated . . . with a view of assisting the digestive process, the pills prescribed will prove very helpful'. After that, the treatment of a mere inflammation of the womb is surely obvious. In addition to rest and localised treatment, this condition is treated by 'a careful regulation of the bowels'. Meanwhile, 'to avoid varicose veins: first, attend to the daily evacuation of the bowels; second, support the pregnant womb by a well-fitting abdominal bandage; and third, do not wear garters'. Finally, mothers were reminded that their sins could be transmitted to their offspring. According to Dr Bell, 'Frequently we find the digestion of the infant at fault from no other cause than that the mother's digestive organs are out of order. She should therefore see that her bowels act regularly every day.'

Considering the terrors of constipation in the 1920s (and it should be remembered that Dr Bell's views were by no means unusual), who can deny the value of an educational system which has ensured that the use of laxatives failed to keep pace with the steep increase in the use of tranquillisers?

Magic pills

Large numbers of people experience powerful effects, beneficial or adverse, when they take inert substances disguised in the form of pills. The nature and determinants of the symbolic value of pill-taking are pre-eminently psychological subjects. Although we are far from achieving a thorough understanding of placebo reactions, we do have some knowledge about the factors which influence the size, nature and direction of such reactions.

In a recent study conducted in a general practice in South London, it was found that more than half of the forty patients receiving these inert placebo tablets (for the reduction of anxiety) complained of unpleasant side-effects.[6] One-quarter said that the tablets had given them headaches, another quarter complained that the tablets interfered with their sleep, or their alertness. Other patients complained that they produced nausea, blurred vision, shakiness and so on. In a second example, from the University of California, three hundred neurotic patients were given one of three types of tranquillisers or an inert tablet throughout the six months of their treatment by psychotherapy. All four groups of patients showed slight improvement over the treatment period and again at a two-year follow-up enquiry. Brill and his colleagues could detect no differences between the improvements registered by the three drug-treated groups and the patients who received placebos.[7] It was also found that the effects of psychotherapy were hardly noticeable, being neither smaller nor greater than those observed in patients who had received the inert tablets.

Our third example, a study carried out on neurotic patients at the Johns Hopkins Medical School in Baltimore, produced a remarkable outcome. Park and Covi were interested in finding out how their patients would respond to a placebo tablet when they were fully informed about its inert contents.[8] Each of the fifteen patients was assessed on his first visit and then given a prescription of placebo. They were also given the following explanation: 'Many people with your kind of condition have also been helped by what are sometimes called "sugar pills", and we feel that a so-called sugar pill may help you too. Do you know what a sugar pill is? A sugar pill is a pill with no medicine in it at all.

I think this pill will help you as it has helped so many others. Are you willing to try this pill?'

Each patient was given a supply of the inert substance in the form of pink capsules 'contained in a small bottle with a label showing the name of the Johns Hopkins Hospital. He was instructed to take the capsules quite regularly, one capsule three times a day at each mealtime.' The researchers saw the patients a week later to re-evaluate their condition and to explore their reactions to having been given a non-active drug.

Fourteen of the fifteen patients kept their second appointment and all but one of them took the prescribed dosage more or less as instructed. Thirteen of them showed improvement.

The magnitude of the improvement can be gauged from the fact that there was a 41 per cent decrease in symptoms. Three of the patients also complained of side-effects which they attributed to the action of the pills. Nine out of the fourteen patients felt that the pill was 'the major factor in their improvement'. The most surprising feature of the result is that improvement occurred even in the patients who knew that the placebo was in fact inert. 'There was no difference in improvement ratings between those eight patients who believed the pills contained placebo and the six patients who believed an active drug was involved.' To cap it all, four of the fourteen patients stated that the placebo pill was 'the most effective ever prescribed for them'.

This particular example of placebo power cannot be attributed to mere credulity. The authors themselves attributed most of the beneficial effect to the enthusiasm with which the participant doctors carried out their task.

As it is so remarkable, this finding needs to be replicated in larger samples, including non-psychiatric groups. As we shall see, there is independent evidence that the attitude of the prescribing doctor to his tablets and the way in which this attitude comes across to the patient are in fact important factors in the patient's reaction to placebos. This, incidentally, is one of the main reasons for the inclusion, in strict clinical trials of drugs and other forms of treatment, of independent assessors and for keeping the participant doctors in ignorance about the tablets that they are prescribing. Failure to provide this type of 'double blind' control would mean biased procedures and assessments that would distort the interpretation of the effects of the treatment.

In an extensive review of current knowledge, one of the most prominent research workers in this field has traced the decline and fall of various medical panaceas.[9] He reminds us that Galen's elaborate book of medicines contained 820 substances—'all worthless'. Nevertheless the grand old man and his numerous disciples administered these substances in various combinations to the great satisfaction of many of their patients. Paradoxically, these physicians probably did help their patients despite the administration of useless and sometimes dangerous medications. Treatments recommended by medical authorities in a confident way that is designed to arouse hope and expectations will frequently have a beneficial outcome. All too often, however, this important factor is ignored. Doctors in particular tend to adopt a defensive position on the question of placebos instead of capitalising on these powerful non-specific contributors to the relief of distress. Shapiro has in fact found that while most physicians admit the occurrence of placebo reactions, they tend to play down their importance in their own medical speciality.[9] So 'surgeons exclude surgery' from the definition of placebo, and 'psychotherapists and psychoanalysts exclude psychotherapy and psychoanalysis'. A greater understanding of placebo reactions would enable doctors to use them to greatest effect in their own fields.

These non-specific, placebo reactions occur not only in drug administration but in virtually all forms of medical treatment.[10] For example, in an experimental study of the treatment of anxiety about speaking in public Paul achieved moderately good results by the skilful use of what he called an attention-placebo condition.[11] His subjects were taken to a sophisticated-looking laboratory in order to engage in a variety of meaningless tasks and measurements, carried out by an efficient and authoritative 'therapist'.

Premature or excessive reliance on placebo tactics is however inadvisable, not least because they are capable of producing adverse effects as well as benefits. As was shown in our first example, a substantial number of people complain of unpleasant side-effects from taking sugar pills. Luckily, the benefits are generally greater and more extensive than the negative reactions. Contrary to the belief of many people, placebo reactions are not necessarily fleeting. In the Californian drug study described on page 96, benefits were derived from the administration of tranquillisers or placebos, and the placebo group were found to have retained their slight improvements at the end of the two-year follow-up period.[7]

As we have already seen, the placebo effect is not necessarily eliminated when the patient is informed about its inert qualities. Another curious fact is that the administration of placebo tablets has been found to maintain people in types of treatment other than drugs. So, for example, in using the bell-and-pad method, Turner and Young found that mothers carried out the doctors' instructions more readily if a placebo was given to the child.[12] Whether one likes it or not, many patients retain a stereotyped view of what medical treatment comprises. Advice, exercises, diets and the rest seem not to be taken as seriously as 'real medicine' —sugar-coated, encapsuled, bottled, and cryptically labelled.

A further complication lies in the fact that in the ordinary course of their work it is difficult for doctors to assess the effects of the drugs they prescribe. For example, in a study of drug effects on patients with inflammatory joint diseases, Joyce found that fifteen out of the twenty patients expressed satisfaction with the phenylbutazone prescribed by Dr B, whereas only five out of eighteen of Dr A's patients felt satisfied when given the same drug.[13] Five of Dr C's patients were most satisfied with a placebo drug but only one of Dr B's patients had this reaction. Joyce notes in passing that had Dr B not participated in this particular trial, phenylbutazone might well have been dismissed as ineffective. The major point however is that had they known the identity of the drugs they were using, it is likely that the three doctors participating would have drawn very different conclusions about the effects of their prescriptions. As we shall see presently, the doctor's expectation of outcome can be crucial in determining the therapeutic effects of the treament. It comes as no surprise, then, to find that uncontrolled studies of therapeutic drug actions are claimed to be effective five times more frequently than independently assessed investigations. Foulds observed that in twenty controlled investigations of therapeutic drug action, success was claimed in only five of them; in fifty-two uncontrolled studies, however, claims for successful drug action were made in forty-three out of the fifty-two studies.[14]

The important part played by the doctor's expectations of success or failure is neatly illustrated in a report by Uhlenhuth and others.[15] Two psychiatrists who differed in their expectations of drug effects were asked to prescribe drugs and placebo tablets to their patients. The patients of the optimistic doctor responded substantially better than did those of the sceptical doctor. The manner in which the doctor introduces and recommends the tablets to the patient is certainly influential in producing the resulting drug effect. On a more mundane level, reactions to drugs have been found to be susceptible to such superficial characteristics as the colour of the tablets, whether they are pills or capsules, the nature of the instructions for administering them and so on. We also know that certain types of people are more likely to react to placebo treatment than others. In medical and surgical patients, as well as in psychiatric patients, placebo responses are more common in sociable, conventional, dependent people, whereas mistrustful and isolated patients tend to show little or no placebo reaction. Anxious patients are more likely to show placebo reactions than non-anxious ones.

An important aspect of the doctor's 'placebo power' is the amount of personal interest which he shows in his patient. This is likely to be associated with the patient's liking for him and hence of the patient's tendency to comply with the doctor's advice and to find his tablets to be effective. Doctors who show little personal interest in their patients are seldom liked by them and their 'placebo power' is diminished.

The doctor's enthusiasm for the treatment which he is recommending appears to enhance its value. This enthusiasm, which has obvious advantages, helps to explain why the innovators of new forms of treatment so often obtain better results than anyone else. Enthusiasm of this kind is probably at the bottom of another interesting therapeutic phenomenon—novel treatments are often found to be more effective than older forms. It is for this reason that doctors are sometimes given the half-serious advice to 'use a new form of treatment while it works'.

The occurrence of placebo reactions is usually regarded as a source of embarrassment. They can however be turned to advantage and used to make treatment and care more resourceful and effective. Recognition of the pervasiveness of placebo effects is a first step in this direction. In time, psychological research will improve our understanding of their nature and enable us to exploit them sensibly. We need not continue to use placebos in the present restricted manner—that is, mainly to provide a safe basis for comparison with new drugs or other treatments. With little extra effort we can increase the power of our pills (and our doctors) by skilful boosting of those qualities and factors which make a non-specific (placebo) contribution to therapy, such as the enthusiasm of doctors and the confidence of patients.

All this calls for greater concentration on psychological factors. The primary need is for intensive research, mainly of a psychological character, into the *determinants* of placebo phenomena. It is essential that this research is broadened to include specialities outside psychiatry. In our view, attention should be shifted towards general-practice medicine and to the selection and effects of non-prescribed medicines.

7 Self-control of bodily functions

Control yourself

When our bodily discomforts or pains reach an intense level we generally first seek the advice of people we are close to, usually relatives and friends. Depending on their reactions (and our discomforts) we might then seek the advice of a doctor. Alternatively, we might decide to do nothing, or take a self-selected medicine, or change our behaviour. This last alternative covers a range of possible actions—taking a rest, drinking less alcohol, eating less (or more), getting more sleep, taking exercise, changing diets, moving house or simply thinking healthy thoughts. Another important possibility, that of changing our behaviour in order to increase *direct* bodily control, has not been taken seriously until very recently. Advancing psychological research has shown that, given appropriate training conditions, we are capable of achieving partial control of bodily functions (e.g. heart rate) which were formerly regarded as being entirely involuntary. Given the necessary support and some good fortune, psychologists may soon find themselves in possession of techniques for teaching bodily self-control— for example, to reduce pain. We may yet see the return, in modern dress, of that popular Victorian prescription—'Exercise self-control.'

Another old adage, 'Know thyself', may also take on amusing new significance as psychologists begin to pay attention to man's *internal* environment. We can expect improvement in our sensitivity to internal events and an expansion of language, made necessary by the need to communicate our internal sensations more precisely and effectively. In time, these scientific advances will influence medical practice—most obviously because the patient's account of his internal sensations and events is the basis of clinical practice.

Some Western doctors and psychologists also have a new interest in acupuncture (particularly in relation to pain) and in meditation. The interest in meditation is more than a romantic longing; it arises from two significant advances made by experimentalists working in the mainstream of psychological research. In the first place, brilliant work by Neal Miller and his colleagues has shown that certain functions of the autonomic nervous system, formerly thought to be beyond deliberate control, can be manipulated in astonishingly precise ways by the actions of the organism concerned. So, for example, a rat can be taught to increase the vasomotor responses of its left ear while those of its right ear continue unchanged (see below, p. 110).[1] The second and related advance comes from experimental attempts to train people to achieve a measure of voluntary control over some of their own bodily functions, such as heart rate. The research directed at increasing self-control relies mainly on a technique called *biofeedback*.

The term refers to procedures in which biological information about a person's functions are 'fed back' to him by technical devices that provide him with an external display of his internal functions, for example, a visual display of heart rate, second by second. This biological information is of course inaccessible under ordinary circumstances and is displayed externally in order to give the patient the means to control some aspects of his bodily function that are otherwise independent of his direct control. The functions which have attracted most attention are heart rate, blood pressure and electrical activity of the brain (EEG) and of the skin, all of which have long been regarded, at least in the West, as being involuntary. It has now been established that under specified conditions a person who is provided with feedback about certain of his bodily functions can learn to control them to some extent.

An example will clarify the procedure. In order to teach a person how to achieve a measure of control over his heart rate, electrodes would be attached to his body and connected to a pulse meter, so that a continuous measure of his heart rate is obtained. This measure is then translated into a visual signal from which he is able to observe the speed of his heart rate, second by second or beat by beat. He is instructed to use this normally inaccessible information to increase or decrease the rate. In some instances he need be given no further information than that simple instruction. More efficient control can be obtained by providing him with some hints, such as the fact that imagining exciting activities will facilitate heart-rate increases and imagining calm and drowsy situations will tend to slow it down. Diagram I below shows how simple the procedure is. Improvements can be made in the form in which the feedback is presented, in the setting or the instructions and so forth but, basically, biofeedback procedures are rather simple.

Research on the clinical application of biofeedback training procedures is beginning to flourish. Some promising early results have been achieved in cases of hypertension, migraine, muscle-contraction headaches and other problems. We may also be on the verge of advances in feedback training that will enable us to ameliorate some of the so-called psychosomatic dis-

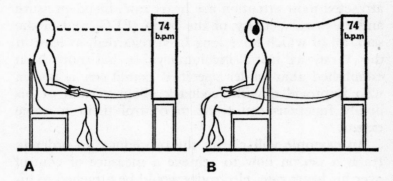

Diagram I   *Acquiring control of cardiac rate*

These two sketches illustrate simple laboratory arrangements for training subjects to acquire control. In the first (A), the subject's cardiac rate is fed into a visual display and he is instructed to increase or decrease his 'score'. In the second (B) his cardiac rate is transformed into an auditory signal which informs him of increases and decreases. Limited short-term changes can be obtained easily but substantial and/or enduring changes are more difficult to achieve (Rachman, 1974).

orders. For example, one can foresee how asthmatics might be trained to achieve proper control over the dilation and contraction of their bronchi.

Two important influences have stimulated the interest in and the application of biofeedback.

1   The first came from research workers who were intrigued by the self-control apparently achieved during meditation. It is held that during transcendental meditation the monk or yogi attains voluntary control over many aspects of his bodily functions which are ordinarily inaccessible. Wenger and Bajchi, for example, described the case of a yogi who was able to perspire from his forehead on command. Another yogi could

106

slow his heart rate to such an extent that little blood was being pumped and no heart sounds could be heard even with a stethoscope.[2] Many other remarkable examples are quoted by Arthur Koestler in his book on India and Japan, *The Lotus and the Robot*.[3] They include some little-known instances of precise control of highly specific digestive functions, achievements which might strike Europeans as being both astonishing and pointless, in equal measure.

Apparently, experienced practitioners of meditation are capable of drawing air into their intestines by voluntary contraction of the anal sphincter. And water can be drawn in through the rectum. Altogether, Koestler found that many yogis have an obsessional interest in bowels, which probably commended them to members of the British Empire such as Dr Bell, as being proper and worthy.

2 The second influence came from a number of psychologists (most notably N. E. Miller) who successfully challenged firmly held beliefs about the capacities of the nervous system. For many years authorities on psychology distinguished between two types of learning and two parts of the nervous system. It was believed that the autonomic nervous system and the central nervous system mediated discrete types of learning. In brief the argument went as follows: Trial and error learning, sometimes called instrumental learning, is mediated by the central nervous system and the responses involved are under voluntary control. In contrast, responses mediated by the autonomic nervous system are involuntary and can only be learned by classical conditioning, a form of learning by association.

Belief in the existence of these two basic types of learning was so strong that workers such as Miller found it difficult to obtain funds and research equipment to examine alternative theories:

> The belief that it is impossible for the stupid autonomic nervous system to exhibit the more sophisticated instrumental learning was so strong that for more than a decade it was extremely hard for me to get any students or even paid assistants to work seriously on the problem. I almost always ended up by letting them work on something they did not think was so preposterous.[4]

In fact, when the experiments (on animals) were attempted they achieved success in training autonomic responses by instrumental learning techniques. Other experimenters then showed that when people are given information about the activity of some aspect of their autonomic nervous system and instructed to vary that activity in order to achieve some reward, these people achieved a degree of control over their autonomic activities, for instance, increasing their heart rate, by a few beats, at will. Thus it appears that, contrary to long-held beliefs, responses mediated by this branch of the nervous system can be manipulated, even voluntarily, after a course of training akin to trial-and-error learning.

Arguments about the relation between types of learning and types of nervous system are of minor interest to clinicians, however. For them it is not so much a question of the types of learning operating, as one of gaining control of previously 'mute', independent response systems. Recent research has yielded information about the factors that appear to be important to the success of biofeedback training procedures. It appears, not surprisingly, that the more accurate and more extensive the information provided to the person about the activity of the response system in question, the greater the degree of control achieved. Continuous feedback of information from the system is usually more effective than discrete pieces of information provided periodically over a training session. There are also data to suggest that the modality of feedback signal can affect the rate of success. So, for example, it has been found that an auditory feedback signal is more effective than a visual signal in lowering forehead muscle tension. The greater the enlightenment given the person about the significance of the feedback and his reactions to it, the better the outcome. Early fears that people might perform less well when they are made aware of the purpose of the training have fortunately not been confirmed. Although there is some evidence to support the idea that acquisition of these skills is facilitated by increasing the frequency of training trials, we have early indications that beyond a certain number of training sessions further progress is noticeably slower.

Animal studies

Some of the most thorough and valuable experimental work has come from Professor Miller's own laboratory. Operating under highly controlled laboratory conditions, learned control of diverse glandular and visceral responses has been achieved. Functions such as heart rate, intestinal motility, blood pressure, skin temperature, urine formation and so on have all been successfully modified. Most of the research has been carried out on rats and it has been necessary to use the drug curare to paralyse temporarily the skeletal muscles in order to rule out the possible influence of muscle activities. This experimental control is coupled with the use of electrical stimulation of the reward centres of the brain, thereby allowing the experimenter to control the rewards given to the animal, contingent on the occurrence of the appropriate bodily reaction (for example, increase or decrease of heart rate). Some of the more remarkable successes include the following experiments. In one instance, heart rate and intestinal contractions were recorded in a group of rats. Half of the rats were rewarded for changes in heart rate and the other half for changes in intestinal contractions. As can be seen in Diagram II, the group rewarded for heart rate increases learned to increase the rate, while the group rewarded for intestinal contractions learned to increase this activity. The specificity of the training effect is shown by the fact that the group rewarded for heart rate increases showed no change in intestinal activity, and, similarly, the group rewarded for changes in intestinal contractions showed no change in cardiac activity. An even more astonishing demonstration of the precision of the learned changes is provided in an experiment on modifying vasomotor responses in rats. Here twelve rats were rewarded for vasodilation of either the right or the left ear. As can be seen in Diagram III, the 'trained' ear showed a striking increase in vasodilation over the untrained ear.

Experiments of this character, many of which have now been supported by research in other laboratories, demonstrate that Miller's conviction was correct. It is possible to modify responses which are mediated through the autonomic nervous system by instrumental learning, that is trial-and-error training. Even extremely subtle and highly specific responses can be modified provided that the physiological changes can be monitored and relayed back to the animal, either directly or indirectly.

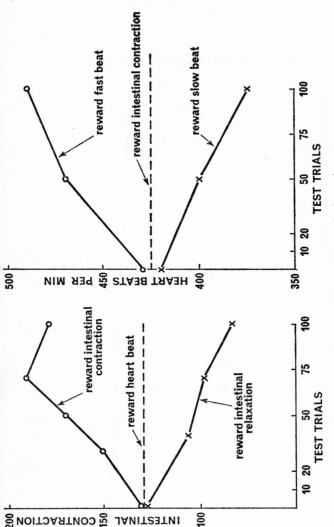

Diagram II *The specificity of learned visceral responses*

Left-hand graph shows intestinal contraction scores. These are seen to increase or decrease in response to rewards given contingent on the occurrence of the desired intestinal responses. When heart rate changes were rewarded, no changes in intestinal contractions occurred. The right-hand graph shows the results obtained from rewarding heart rate increases or decreases. The rewarding of intestinal changes produced no alterations in heart rate. Adapted from N. E. Miller, *Science*, Vol. 163, 1969.

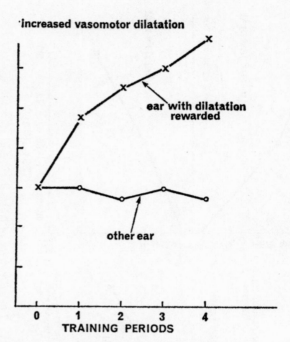

increased vasomotor dilatation

ear with dilatation rewarded

other ear

0   1   2   3   4
TRAINING PERIODS

Diagram III   *The specificity of a learned vasomotor response*

Here the left and right ears of the same rat were trained, by the application of contingent rewards, to respond in different (vaso-motor) directions. The left ear showed increased vasodilation and the right ear vasoconstriction or no change. This remarkable vasomotor specificity was repeated on six rats. Adapted from N. E. Miller, *Science*, Vol. 163, 1969.

Human studies

Most of the results on humans have been obtained by studying groups of healthy undergraduates under laboratory conditions. A number of experimenters have reported success in attaining self-control of heart rate to the extent of increasing or decreasing the rate by as many as ten beats per minute, as well as achieving reductions in the variability of heart rate.[5, 6] Overall, it appears that heart-rate acceleration is easier to learn than deceleration, at least in healthy subjects. This may well reflect the lower resting-level of heart rate in normal subjects—there is less scope for a decrease. It is worth noting, however, that although the experimental changes are of the order of three to five beats per minute on average, they are rarely large enough to be of clinical significance. More substantial changes have in fact been produced in individual cases but this seems to require many training sessions. Headrick and others described a person who achieved an average increase of thirty beats per minute after five training sessions, but he became so tense and uneasy that the training had to be discontinued.[7] It should be noted that, in general, smaller changes of rate are rarely noticed—except, of course, on the specially designed display equipment.

Concentrating on the learned control of blood pressure, Shapiro and his colleagues have demonstrated small but significant increases and decreases in both systolic and diastolic blood pressure under feedback arrangements.[8, 9, 10] These changes occur independently of heart-rate changes. Recently they succeeded in demonstrating that people can learn to produce integrated changes in blood pressure and heart rate if the reward is made whenever both responses occur simultaneously. Even more striking, they have also produced non-integrated changes, in which blood pressure and heart rate are made to vary independently.

Equivocal results have emerged from attempts to achieve self-control of electrodermal fluctuations (changes in the electrical resistance of the skin), perhaps because of the considerable methodological problems involved in working with this fragile measure.[11] Although the self-control of most skeletal muscles has never been at issue, the voluntary control of the basic unit of motor control (comprising an effector neurone and the attached muscle fibres), was thought to be unattainable. It has now been achieved by the use of biofeedback techniques. Basmajian has shown that under suitable feedback conditions, a person can learn sufficient control to allow him to generate rhythmic firing and drum-beat rhythms of one of these discrete motor units.[12]

Basmajian has also reported another surprising finding—one with clinical implications. He found that with the help of feedback procedures, absolute levels of muscle action potential can be made to drop very close to zero levels—or no muscle tension at all. This suggests that conditions in which heightened tension is implicated (and there are many of them, e.g. back pain, headaches, etc.) may respond to muscle relaxation by training, using conventional or biofeedback methods. Some early successes have already been claimed (e.g. Budzynski and Stoyva[13]).

Electrical activity of the brain, particularly the alpha band of wave activity (8–13 c.p.s.), has also been modified by the use of biofeedback techniques. This alpha band occurs in states of relaxed wakefulness, and is most pronounced when the eyes are closed.[14] It appears that people can learn to increase alpha activity or suppress it at will, irrespective of whether their eyes are open or closed.[15] These findings have interested psychologists, not only because of the demonstration of specific learned control of such a complex neurophysiological process, but also because they might lead to a new approach to the study of mood.

The excitement has unfortunately led some writers to speculate rather unwisely about what might be achieved. It has been suggested, for example, that one might be able to change mood states by having a subject 'turn on' a certain cerebral rhythm. It is surely misleading to conclude, as Maslow has done, that we can now 'teach people how to feel happy and serene'.[16] These exaggerated claims are unfounded, not least because it is most unlikely that gross changes in the electric-wave activity of the brain (EEG) can ever reflect the myriad subjective moods.

In summary, biofeedback techniques can be used to achieve a measure of self-control over what were previously believed to be fully autonomous bodily functions. This may not be news in Benares, but it generates enthusiasm in London and it may soon be put to clinical use.

Clinical applications

It is hoped that these techniques may ultimately become useful tools in the treatment of psychosomatic disorders as well as chronic conditions such as cardiac dysfunctions, high blood pressure, headaches and so on. Significant feedback effects have been obtained in laboratories, but can they be reproduced in a clinical setting? Might not the existing abnormality of function interfere with learned changes? Can we induce changes large enough to produce clinically significant improvement? In sum, can we make the transition from trivial and transient laboratory changes to substantial, enduring clinical improvement?

Although the applications have so far been limited to case studies or pilot projects, the early results are none the less encouraging. Here are some examples. Engel and Weiss tried to obtain a significantly improved control of irregularities of heart beat (cardiac arrhythmia) in a group of eight patients suffering from a specific dysfunction of the heart (premature ventricular contractions).[17] The results, which are shown for each individual patient, show some striking changes in electrocardiographic (ECG) rhythm during the sessions. After a controlled period, each patient was taught heart-rate acceleration followed by deceleration, finishing off with a number of sessions in which they were taught to alternate increases and decreases of heart rate within a circumscribed period. Each patient had to maintain his heart rate within a certain range, and the feedback arrangements ensured that he knew whenever he exceeded or failed to reach the range. All the patients acquired some degree of control over their heart rate. Five of the eight showed a more regular heart beat on at least one of the three training conditions, and four of the five were able to maintain these changes after the experiment. One patient even succeeded in retaining his new skill for as long as twenty-one months.

The application of biofeedback techniques to the lowering of systolic blood pressure in patients with hypertension has also been fruitful.[9] The results show learned decreases in blood pressure in six of the seven patients, but the changes were not consistently associated with the slowing of the heart rate. As hypertension is more closely associated with diastolic blood pressure,

116

it is hoped that Shapiro and his colleagues will attempt to replicate the control of diastolic blood pressure which they have already achieved in people with normal functioning, in a group of hypertensive patients—particularly as they have already had success in altering systolic pressure.[9]

Another valuable application of biofeedback was started by Budzynski and his colleagues.[18] They have been attempting to control tension headaches by training their patients to relax their muscles. These headaches are assumed to result from sustained contraction of neck and scalp muscles (see Chapter 4). In their study, the frontalis muscle alone was monitored, presumably because they hoped that this muscle was involved in the headaches experienced by all their patients. They did in fact find that the basal levels of muscle tension were exceptionally high in the headache group, equal to nearly twice that of healthy people. In a pilot treatment study on five chronic headache cases, their patients were given an auditory tone, the frequency of which was proportional to the muscle tension of the frontalis muscle. Encouraging results were obtained: it appears that even these chronic cases can be taught to voluntarily lower the tension of the frontalis muscle and this decrease can be sustained in their everyday life. The frequency and intensity of headaches declined with the reduction in muscle-tension levels. In these cases the effective results were achieved in four to eight weeks. Although this preliminary study lacks adequate controls and consists of only a small number of patients, it marks an important start in the management of an extremely common disorder, by methods other than drugs. As it is unlikely that the stress conditions which are considered to be instrumental in producing tension headaches can ever be eliminated, the self-control designed

117

to give the sufferer a means of reducing tension, and hence the pain, is particularly welcome.

Yet another interesting application of biofeedback methods was reported by Jacob and Felton, who worked with ten patients suffering from injuries of the upper trapezius muscle (see diagram on p. 65).[19] They compared this group with ten physically normal people, and found that their injured group had a greatly heightened basal level of muscular tension and appeared to be unable to relax the trapezius muscle by ordinary means. When provided with a visual feedback display of the activity of the muscle (myoelectric impulses) on an oscilloscope however, a remarkable change occurred. Under instructions to relax, the tension levels of the patients dropped rapidly to those of the uninjured group. This large, early response is almost characteristic of biofeedback applications and will need to be explained; it may indicate that the changes are different from the more gradual improvements typical of training in other skills. No information on the subjective effects experienced by the patients after such a marked change was supplied, nor can we be sure of the durability of the changes. None the less, we can take seriously the challenge that these results are promising for rehabilitation and training programmes in which interfering muscle groups retard corrective progress. Nor is it impossible to imagine the successful application of these techniques in helping some patients to regain the use of impaired muscles.

Although it has been suggested that certain types of epilepsy may be brought under control by teaching patients how to suppress voluntarily the epileptic 'spikes' (sharp irregularities of brain-wave activity) no clinical research reports have yet appeared. So far there have been few reports of attempts to achieve self-control of electrical activity of the brain for clinical purposes. At McGill University investigations have begun in the use of self-control procedures to enhance alpha activity of the brain, with the aim of thereby reducing chronic pain (as in low back pain and arthritis).

It can be seen that a useful beginning has been made in applying biofeedback techniques to medical problems. We are approaching the stage of carrying out well-controlled clinical investigations. The opportunities for psychologists, particularly psychophysiologists, are considerable.

Outstanding issues

At this point in a rapidly expanding field such as biofeedback, it is worth delineating some of the issues that need to be clarified, in both the laboratory and the clinic. So far research workers have been mainly concerned with demonstrating the acquisition of learned control, over relatively few trials and commonly within a single training session. The magnitude of the effect has been less important than its occurrence. The aim has been to obtain effects significantly greater than those observed in the appropriately chosen control group (for example, those who receive either no feedback at all or incorrect feedback). However, there is no longer any doubt that these bodily systems can be modified and that feedback arrangements provide a simple and effective basis for modification. The outstanding problems are how to achieve the best conditions for encouraging self-control, how to enlarge the changes and how to retain control even after withdrawal of the external feedback signals.

With regard to the first issue, experiments need to be performed in which the length of both the trials themselves and the intervals between them are systematically varied. It would also be helpful if the experiment reports in future provided more detail than simple average effects. We also need systematic investigations of the effects of varying amounts and types of feedback information. As mentioned earlier, the type of feedback —visual or auditory—may also be a factor worth consideration, as people almost certainly differ in the way that they can best take in information about their own bodies.

The question of the durability of the effects is of central interest, especially in application to medical problems. The aim would be to teach a lasting skill that can be used whenever the need arises. To date, little attention has been given to promoting effects that persist after training sessions. Such factors as the number of trials, the number of sessions and the importance of instructions appear to be obviously relevant and will need detailed study. It may also be that greater skill can be taught by patients practising 'turning on' their control skills in the face of either imaginary stresses or of graded presentations of stressful material. In other words, the desensitisation approach that has proved to be so useful in psychiatric applications might be reshaped to teach self-control in precisely those situations of stress where it is ordinarily difficult to employ. This is a move from a concern for control of basal states to a greater concern for the control of responses under stress.

As we have seen, most of our knowledge derives from the laboratory and there is always some doubt about the feasibility of transfer to the clinical situation. However, few of the clinical case reports give support to any suggestion that learning is more difficult for patients. It may even be found that the decrease of abnormally elevated functions is easier for the clinical groups to achieve, because there is more room for change than is the case in a normally functioning group. On the other hand, we also have good reason to expect large individual differences in subjective estimates of pain and tension, the amount of change detectable by different subjects and the amount of change needed to modify the symptoms.

The growth of biofeedback techniques was made possible by the development of equipment that adequately senses, amplifies and projects the activity of biological systems. Further progress will depend on the efficiency, size and mobility of this equipment. One can already foresee that some patients will ultimately need portable miniature systems that can be used whenever needed in daily life to ensure durable changes.

A great deal of work needs to be undertaken in order to develop biofeedback into a practical clinical procedure, and this branch of clinical psychology alone could absorb the efforts of an entire year's crop of graduates.

Suitable medical problems

It is easy to overestimate the value of a new technique and there is a general tendency to recommend new methods for all existing ailments. Even at this early stage it is worth trying to clarify the types of disorder that seem to us best suited to a biofeedback approach.

The most appropriate and clear-cut use for biofeedback is in the modification of disorders of function that are (*a*) localised by specific complaints, (*b*) objectively quantifiable and (*c*) under minimal, if any, control by the sufferer. This definition includes a range of medical problems. Suitable examples include muscular disorders such as tension headaches, low back pain and specific motor disabilities. It might be predicted that migraine could be investigated and possibly treated by modifying the constriction and dilation of arteries. Psychosomatic disorders such as ulcers might be ameliorated by teaching control of acidity levels in the stomach or, more simply, by reducing stomach tension levels. Subject to technical advances, asthma might be modified by teaching control of bronchial constriction and dilation. Some cardio-vascular conditions have already received attention and the technique looks particularly promising for people suffering from hypertension.

A second major use for biofeedback techniques is in the production of changes in general state—in the hope that they will act to inhibit certain chronic complaints. As these changes in general state are ordinarily outside voluntary control, chronic sufferers might be helped if they could learn to turn on alternative states, such as deep relaxation, by making use of feedback from one or more bodily systems.

8 Reducing health risks by self-control

Psychological factors play a large part in over-eating and smoking, both forms of behaviour which carry health risks. Contrary to what we often prefer to believe, smoking is not a 'minor vice' but a potentially lethal form of behaviour.[1] Excessive eating also is more hazardous than is generally realised.[2] In theory, both types of behaviour are open to modification by psychological means. In practice, it is sad to admit, psychologists have not reported satisfactory progress in spite of the intense research conducted over the last few years. If they fail in their attempts to modify these forms of immoderate behaviour, the credibility of their claims for a larger role in the Health Service, as argued in this book and elsewhere, will suffer. Psychologists need to do better, but can they? In this chapter we discuss some of the methods explored, the reasons for their relative failure and the likelihood of future success.

We can anticipate one of our arguments by stating that psychologists are already in a position to achieve partial, but useful and fairly prompt, success by the simple introduction of a new tactic. Instead of devoting all their efforts to changing the behaviour of smokers, psychologists could redirect their aim and spend more time attempting to change the behaviour of the doctors. In this way, they could help to achieve great benefits in the short term. Although our recommendation would have no effect on resistant smokers, who either cannot or will not respond to simple measures, there is good

123

reason to suppose that a large number of smokers would be helped. Here are our reasons for advocating this redistribution of effort. In Chapter 1 we pointed out that there will never be an adequate number of psychologists to justify clinical work based exclusively on person-to-person interactions. We need to develop methods of psychological action which are applicable on a group basis. The problem of smoking provides one such excellent opportunity. Any psychological technique for reducing smoking which is applicable only on a one-to-one basis, no matter how successful, would make little impact on the problem—bearing in mind that slightly over half the adults in Britain smoke. Most psychological methods of control can, of course, be modified for group application. In the case of smoking, however, an even more economical use of psychological expertise would involve changing the behaviour of the doctors.

According to survey findings only 20 per cent of patients report that their doctors have ever advised them to give up smoking.[3, 4] We also know from Russell's review that a doctor's advice is one of the most effective means of persuading smokers to abstain.[5] Consequently, if psychologists used their skills in persuading doctors to always give such advice and guide them as to the most effective content and style of such advice, they would more than earn their keep.

It will be objected that the second part of this suggestion begs the question. What constitutes 'effective content and style' of persuasive medical advice against smoking? Although we acknowledge the difficulty, it is our opinion that if the problems are stated in this novel way they are more likely to yield solutions. As we shall see, the main thrust of psychological research has been towards the direct modification of the smoker's behaviour. We know of no systematic attempts to change the practices of doctors and there has been insufficient interest in how and why their advice can be so successful.

If the question is asked why *psychologists* are needed to put this proposal into action, the reply is double-barrelled. In the first place, despite the many campaigns against smoking and the vast number of medical articles on the subject, only 20 per cent of the patients who responded in the survey mentioned above had been advised by their doctors to give up smoking. Presumably this implies that even if we assume that all practising doctors in this country are aware of the medical risks involved in continuous smoking (and we can safely make this assumption), for some undetected reasons this knowledge has not changed their behaviour towards their patients to any marked degree. Secondly, the delivery and evaluation of persuasive communications fall within the province of psychology. Although the subject needs a great deal of development, we have some facts and findings which would be helpful in any attempt to persuade doctors to advise against smoking (see Chapter 2).

In the longer term, we need to increase our understanding of the nature and causes of smoking and to develop practical and effective treatment methods, particularly for those patients who cannot or will not respond to their doctor's advice or who relapse after a period of abstinence.

Russell, among others, has forcefully put the case that smoking should be regarded as a form of drug dependence and accordingly treated with the same degree of seriousness.[5, 6] It is pointed out that the two most worrying groups of drug-dependent people, alcoholics and drug-addicts, include an extraordinarily high proportion of smokers: 99 per cent of drug-addicts and 92 per cent of alcoholics—as opposed to 56 per cent in the general population. Similarities are shown between the consequences of withdrawal from smoking and withdrawal from these other two main types of drug dependence. In all three cases it is followed by psychological distress and physiological disturbance, including sleep disorders and cardio-vascular disruptions. Moreover, the relapse rates in all three types of dependence follow the same pattern.

Smoking usually starts in a social setting, before the age of twenty, and if an adolescent smokes only three or four cigarettes it is more or less certain that he will continue to smoke for several decades. The point is made dramatically by Russell:

> In the prevailing social climate it is only intravenous drugs which have anything like the dependence-producing potential of cigarette smoking, and it may be no coincidence that the absorption of nicotine through the lungs during smoking is about as rapid and efficient as the junkie's fix.[6]

Apparently the four most important influences on those starting to smoke are the number of one's friends who do so, permissive parental attitudes towards smoking, desire for adulthood and an absence of fear of getting lung cancer. Although the large majority of smokers express the desire to cut down or cut out their smoking, only a small percentage (roughly 18 per cent) achieve success. The successful abstainers tend to be over the age of thirty and have fears about their health. Among the large number of those who attempt to give up, 37 per cent relapse within one year, but those who persist for two years stand roughly a 3-in-4 chance of succeeding. The overall tendency is for former smokers, whether treated or not, to relapse. Although three-quarters of all smokers express a desire to stop, less than one-quarter succeed in achieving their aim.

Psychological research into the factors which encourage a smoker to continue has uncovered some interesting information. Even though the *physiological* effects of smoking are stimulating, many smokers experience and report a calming psychological effect. There is evidence that smoking induces not only calmness but can also help to dampen some of the unpleasant psychological feelings experienced during stress. These findings are consistent with the observation that long-term smokers were more anxious during early adulthood than non-smokers.[7] An elaborate argument relating smoking to personality has been developed by Eysenck.[8] Starting from the premise that extraverts suffer from under-arousal of the cortex, he links this major dimension of personality to the arousing effects of smoking. The deduction that extraverts are more likely than introverts to be continuous smokers has been confirmed—they apparently derive satisfying increases in central stimulation from smoking. As smoking is also capable of producing the calming psychological effects referred to earlier, a proportion of the over-aroused introverts also smoke. In sum, Eysenck argues that smoking is 'maintained because it is an artificial aid in producing a preferred level of arousal'.

Medical and other assistance

Anti-smoking campaigns have had little permanent success, but distinct, although brief, reductions in cigarette consumption do occur in the wake of almost all campaigns. One of the few exceptions to the general observation that the effects of these campaigns are transitory is the example of British doctors who have achieved a permanent decrease in cigarette consumption and in the prevalence of smoking since the publication of the report on smoking by the Royal College of Physicians. Anti-smoking treatment provided at special clinics tends to produce an immediate success rate of anything from 30 per cent to 85 per cent, but this is quickly followed by wholesale relapse. Thus, with few exceptions the effects of clinic interventions are transitory. Commenting on the failure of the pharmaceutical profession to provide an adequate anti-smoking drug, Bernstein deplores the 'dismal picture presented by lobeline research', the most widely recommended and used form of anti-smoking drug.[9]

Persistent smokers have been subjected to many different experiments designed to help them overcome the habit, but with relatively little success. These methods, which range from role-playing to aversion therapy, produce similar results—comparable to those achieved by sugar pills. None achieves more than a temporary reduction in smoking. The use of behavioural self-control techniques and of contracting programmes have been a little disappointing.* Nor have methods designed to change attitudes been as effective as had been hoped; they have, incidentally, helped to confirm that even when the smoker's attitude is successfully changed he will not necessarily change his behaviour accordingly, if at all.[10] Nor indeed is a favourable change in attitude a prerequisite for satisfactory change in behaviour. It is a little dispiriting to have to report that the small successes which have been achieved in applying psychologi-

* The results of a large study on 416 smokers counselled by ten psychologists at the Max Planck Institute in Munich, under the direction of Dr Brengelmann, have not yet been published but they offer some encouragement. The best results were achieved with self-control programmes and aversion therapy, alone or in combination.

cal methods of control to smoking are all of the aversive type. The administration of mild to moderate electric shocks to patients at various points in the chain of smoking behaviour was reasonably successful in Russell's study.[11] He tried the method on fourteen smokers referred from a clinic dealing with chest ailments. Application of the electrical aversion method produced a rapid reduction in smoking in the majority of patients and long-term abstention in six of the nine patients who completed the course—these six were still abstinent one year after completion of treatment. There were three relapses within six months of successful treatment and five of the patients decided to discontinue treatment before achieving successful reduction. If it is objected that the sample size in this study is too small and that in any event the patients were specially selected and presumably well-motivated, one can only agree that more studies of this kind would be valuable.

Another aversive technique involves the delivery of blasts of hot, smoky air into the face of the smoker while he smokes. After some discouraging early reports, this method has clocked up some recent successes and appears to repay further study. A third form of aversive therapy which can claim a small degree of support is called satiation. In this method the smoker is required to smoke rapidly and excessively for prolonged periods. The effect of this is to produce a strong distaste for and even aversion towards cigarettes. The problem here as with other methods is in ensuring that the effects are more than transient. We are not yet in possession of sufficient information on which to decide whether any or all of these aversive techniques can be shaped into effective methods for reducing or stopping smoking for satisfactorily long periods. We are, however, in a position to say that they are among the more promising of a host of largely ineffective psychological procedures which have been used, and that they are therefore worthy of further research.

Few of the considerably more elaborate psychological methods have achieved greater success than the advice of doctors to their patients that it is in their interest to stop smoking. Reviewing the evidence, Russell points out that in one study half of all the people who successfully gave up smoking on grounds of health said that they had done so on the direct advice of their doctors.[4] In an American study, medical advice given on a single visit produced a substantial and lasting reduction in cigarette consumption in one-third of the sample of patients. In Britain, nearly half of a group of patients attending a chest clinic stopped smoking for at least three months after being given routine advice, and Williams, working with a similar type of patient, obtained a high rate of cooperation and a remarkably good overall result.[12] No less than 23 per cent of the group gave up smoking for the whole of a six-month follow-up period, immediately after a single interview. A further 30 per cent gave up smoking for the same duration after receiving additional advice in subsequent interviews.

These are encouraging results, particularly when it is remembered that the advice given was of a fairly simple and routine kind. In none of these studies were elaborate or systematic measures taken. On the other hand, it is probable that these patients, many of them with chest ailments, had strong reasons for following the advice. It is unlikely that similarly high success rates would be attained by simple, routine advice given to a randomly selected group of patients.

The discouraging results obtained by many of the psychological programmes designed to increase self-control led Raw to suggest that greater stress should be placed on comprehensive external controls.[18] In psychological research this distinction between internal and external control has been introduced in analysing excessive eating, and it may well be that analysing smoking along these lines would prove profitable. As a minimum, it would be interesting to know whether smokers, like excessive eaters, are stimulated by external cues to overindulge themselves—for instance, being offered cigarettes. If it could be shown that many or most smokers are strongly influenced by such external factors, it would follow that modification programmes should include attempts to remove or reduce the presence of these cues. Another trend emerging in the research on smoking control is the increasing emphasis placed on the patient's motivation to stop. This movement is strengthened by the fact that almost all forms of intervention, from aversive control to sugar pills, are capable of producing moderate, if short-lived, changes. It is widely believed that one of the main contributors to these non-specific changes is the intention and desire to stop smoking. Needless to say, the examination and analysis of these complex concepts will require a great deal of time and effort. It is hopefully anticipated that a better understanding of the motivation to give up smoking will ultimately help us to come to grips with the very great number of people who fail to complete the course in anti-smoking campaigns or procedures.

It should not be thought that the limited progress made in developing effective psychological techniques for producing smoking abstinence carries a message of unrelieved pessimism. Some methodological advances have been made[9] and some obstacles and difficulties have been removed. For example, improved methods of data collection have been developed, a wide range of non-specific factors in smoking control have been identified and some important clues to the nature of the motivational factors have been detected.

Minimum effort, maximum effect

Medical practitioners have a powerful weapon in the campaign against smoking but have not yet chosen to exercise it fully. Given that at present the method which produces the best results is a doctor's advice, and that up to one in three patients will respond positively to a clear medical warning on the subject, 'the minimum effort' required is a systematic exploitation of the power of medical practitioners. 'The maximum effect' which one can reasonably expect is that up to 30 per cent of the smoking population might be persuaded to at least reduce their cigarette consumption by a clear warning administered by a familiar and trusted doctor, preferably during a period of illness. Naturally, the number of people who could be expected in practice to respond satisfactorily to this approach would fall short of 30 per cent of the adult smoking population, but even so it might exceed a million. This leaves a substantial number of people who will continue to smoke unless other and more successful methods can be developed. As we have seen, so far it is the aversive techniques which show most promise. It is obvious that both the direct method of treating smoking by psychological intervention and the indirect method of persuading and then changing the behaviour of medical practitioners, need to be gone into with great care. As a priority it might be best to concentrate on the development of the most persuasive forms of communication for use by medical practitioners.

In regard to methods of direct treatment, the outstanding problems are how to enlist and maintain the cooperation of smokers and how, once abstinence has been achieved, the disappointingly high relapse rate can be cut. In all this, a greater appreciation of the motives which operate in both smokers and in those who are cured is badly needed. We need clarification of the causes of smoking, which, it is to be hoped, will prepare the ground for wide-scale preventive measures.

Obesity

Excessive eating, like smoking and regrettably many other activities, is pleasurable but potentially harmful. From a psychologist's point of view both habits can be construed as problems of inadequate self-control. Although attempts to increase self-control through psychological means have not met with success in anti-smoking clinics, modest successes have been achieved in reducing obesity. How can we account for the difference? A marked possibility is that raised by Russell, who has argued that smoking is best regarded as a form of drug dependence. There are other differences as well.

Unlike eating, smoking is a superfluous activity; the health risks associated with smoking are the result of indulgence, while those associated with obesity arise from over-indulgence. In attempting to control smoking one aims for abstinence, whereas the aim in eating-control is to achieve moderation. Another difference is that obesity is caused by a combination of factors—excessive (or unwise) eating and insufficient exercise. Hence, attempts to reduce weight should preferably address themselves to decreasing or changing food intake, while increasing physical exercise. Many of the popular methods of slimming do include both elements, and for numbers of people with minor weight problems self-initiated and self-monitored attempts bring satisfactory results. Obese people, however, experience far greater difficulty. Their own attempts to reduce weight are not often successful and medical methods are inadequate. This discouraging state of affairs was summarised by Stunkard, a prominent authority on the subject, who concluded that 'most obese persons will not remain in treatment and of those that remain in treatment, most will not lose weight, and of those who do lose weight, most will regain it'.[14]

As we shall see, some progress has now been made in the use of psychological methods for reducing weight, but in the case of the truly obese person the weight losses have been of statistical rather than clinical significance. While in no way wishing to discourage further attempts to provide psychological solutions, it is as well to keep in mind the possibility that severe obesity may have a mainly physiological basis and therefore be more amenable to physiological remedies. The uncomfortably close behavioural similarities between obese people and obese rats suffering from induced physiological disturbances have been described and analysed with admirable clarity by Schachter.[15] He has also been responsible for conducting fascinating research on obese people; his main conclusion is that they are excessively 'stimulus bound'. That is, their eating behaviour is determined mainly by the sight and availability of food—in contrast to people of average weight whose eating is determined mainly by internal cues, particularly stomach contractions or distension. Obese people experience hunger in a way that 'has almost nothing to do with the state of (their) gut'. In a series of clever experiments Schachter has found that fat people tend to eat whatever tasty food is in sight, even after a meal, whereas other people tend to eat only until they feel full.[16] Although fat people tend to eat fewer meals, they generally eat more, and more quickly. They are however less inclined to expend effort in order to eat (e.g. they prefer forks and spoons to chopsticks when eating Chinese food!) and are *less* likely to complain of hunger when there is no food. This last observation, consistent with Schachter's thesis that obese people are stimulus-bound, has been put to good use in designing behaviour-modification programmes.

Recently, psychologists have begun to pay more attention to the problem of weight reduction, partly as a clinical problem in its own right and partly because it provides a useful analogue for research into psychological techniques for increasing self-control. The aversive conditioning methods which have yielded some positive results in controlling smoking have proved to be disappointing when applied to problems of weight control.[2] Other techniques of behaviour modification, with the exceptions to be described presently, have also produced discouraging results. The most promising results have in fact been achieved by systematic application of self-control programmes, and lately Stunkard endorsed them favourably.[17] In a recent review of progress he said that 'these programmes have been used to compare behaviour modification with a variety of alternate treatment methods. Every one of eight such studies has reported results favouring behaviour modification, an unusual example of unanimity in this heterogeneous and complex disorder.' These studies have characteristically relied on weight changes as the main indicator of success or failure, and while it is true that the studies referred to (and others reported more recently) all report significant reductions in weight, they were not unqualified successes. The actual amounts of weight lost were not large in absolute terms; few of the programmes achieved the goal of producing extensive and lasting losses in weight.

The first comprehensive weight control programme was introduced by Ferster in 1962,[18] developed by Stuart[19, 20] and tested by several other psychologists. The construction of the programmes has been influenced by the work of Schachter who, as we have seen, argues that obese people are more influenced by external cues than are their thinner fellows. Considerable emphasis is therefore placed on the importance of ensuring that the obese person keeps his food in a specific place (e.g. the kitchen) and eats at restricted times. Additionally, special techniques were introduced to help people to eat more slowly, chew smaller portions, pause between mouthfuls and so on. The purpose of these instructions is to help the subject achieve greater control over the act of eating. In order to encourage and then maintain this new style of eating, the subjects are placed on a points system. Exercise of the suggested procedures during and between meals earns a predetermined number of points which are then converted into money and donated by the subject to his favourite charity. Administration of the treatment programme requires between six and ten visits spread over three to eight weeks, followed by monthly follow-up consultations. Before the self-management programme starts, the participants are required to keep detailed records of the size and time of their meals and other circumstances of their eating habits. These data are analysed and used in the construction of the individual subject's programme. It is worth noticing, in passing, that the act of carrying out this self-monitoring activity is usually followed by a clear although modest reduction in eating. (Smokers also reduce consumption when asked to record each cigarette smoked.) The exercises designed to reduce eating habits are supplemented by physical exercises, carried out daily if possible. Successful completion of these exercises is rewarded on the same system of points.

This general approach was used by Penick, Stunkard and their collaborators in a treatment trial involving thirty-two obese patients.[21] Over half of the patients who participated in the programme lost more than twenty pounds and 13 per cent of them lost more than forty pounds. These losses were significantly greater than those achieved by a matched control group of patients treated in the traditional way. The persistence of the improvements as seen at the six-month follow-up time is a particularly encouraging feature of this report, bearing in mind that all too often in the past apparently successful weight-reduction programmes have been quickly followed by relapses.

Another common weakness of many forms of treatment for obese patients is the high attrition rate. It is not unusual to find that more people give up the treatment prematurely than stay the course. Until the advent of these new behavioural self-control programmes, it was unfortunately the case that therapists found it easier to lose patients than pounds. Although Stunkard's optimistic review of recent progress is not misplaced, at least three important obstacles need to be overcome before the new methods can be widely recommended. We need to increase the power of the programmes so that the amount of weight lost reaches clinically significant levels, to take special measures to ensure that relapses are kept to a minimum, and finally to maintain the active cooperation of a far greater proportion of our patients.

9 Psychiatric psychology

Most clinical psychologists are still dealing with problems of abnormal behaviour. Courses in clinical psychology are mainly psychiatric in content, the journals publish mostly psychiatric articles and psychologists for the most part practise psychiatric psychology. Indeed, many are still employed in departments of psychiatry. Before the expansion from psychiatry into other branches of the health services alters the style and purpose of clinical psychology, it might be enlightening to examine the results achieved by the collaboration between the two disciplines, with a view to future developments.

The test era

In the first place, what contributions have psychologists made to the development of psychiatry? Although they include the introduction of some practical measures, to be described presently, we agree with the view that the most useful psychological contribution was 'ideological'. The post-war influx into clinical psychology of rigorously trained experimental psychologists provided welcome support for those psychiatrists who were advocating the introduction of stricter scientific standards into their subject. There can be little argument that the standards and methodology of psychiatry have improved over the past two decades, despite some lingering desires for a return to the confines of nineteenth century Vienna. The balance has shifted from excessive speculation towards increasing reliance on empirical findings.

On the practical side, the early clinical psychologists were bogged down by the hard-won success of their intelligence tests. For a few decades their colleagues in psychiatry continued to pepper them with request forms reading 'IQ test please'. Years of 'test-bashing' produced a dislike of testing that was only partly mitigated by the distractions of Rorschach ink-blot cards, Thematic Apperception Tests (TAT), Minnesota Multiphasic Personality Inventories and other finery. The projective tests, such as the Rorschach, with their promise of providing mental X-rays, have been a failure[1, 2] but the new generation of psychometric tests do earn their keep. Tests of intelligence, after a period of excessive use, now have a valuable if limited place in educational and psychiatric work.

The story of the Rorschach Test, illustrative of the fate of other projective tests as well, is sobering. The Test consists of ten cards each depicting an ink-blot. The cards are presented to the patient in a fixed sequence and he is asked to respond freely to them and describe his perceptions. These are classified and then interpreted and frequently given weight in reaching psychiatric diagnoses. There are, however, convincing reasons for concluding that the Test is neither reliable nor valid. Consider the fate of only one aspect of the frequently complex types of interpretation placed on the subject's account of his perceptions. Great significance was attached to the person's reaction to the last few cards, which contain colour. Literally hundreds of journal papers were written on the interpretation of reactions to the colour on these cards, but recently research has shown that the test results are unchanged when specially produced achromatic cards are substituted for the coloured ones. On a broader scale, the important and ambitious study reported by Little and Shneidman in 1959 examined the validity of the conclusions drawn from patients' responses to projective tests.[3] They obtained the services of acknowledged experts in projective test analysis and compared their independently determined interpretations of test protocols obtained from normal people, neurotic and psychotic patients. They also compared conclusions drawn from the Rorschach Test data with those deduced from other sources, including tests.

The findings revealed such extensive and serious disagreements and errors in diagnosis as to bring into question the use of the Rorschach Test on any patient, at any time. Despite their brave attempts to draw some comfort from the study, Little and Shneidman suggested that 'diagnostic labels based upon blind analyses of protocols may be quite wide of the mark and the present analysis indicates that judges may not even be shooting at the same target' [p. 11]. As we shall see, this is an under-statement.

The first test participant was *normal*. Like all the others, he completed three projective tests (including the Rorschach) and one other psychological test. His results on each of the four tests were interpreted by four experts, giving a total of sixteen independent diagnoses. These judges turned up no less than ten different pathological labels! He was described variously as suffering from schizophrenia, anxiety neurosis, hysteria, psychopathic personality, brain damage, character neurosis, homosexual tendencies and possible alcoholism. The next person, also normal, received *twelve* different diagnostic labels out of the sixteen offered. They included conversion hysteria, compulsive neurosis, homosexuality, neurotic depression, anxiety neurosis, character neurosis, schizoid character with depressive trends and so on. At the other extreme, participant number eleven was suffering from schizophrenia. Although nine of the sixteen diagnosis were correct in this case, he was variously described as being normal, neurotic, immature and suffering from hysteria. The tenth person, also suffering from schizophrenia, produced even less satisfactory responses from the experts. Three of the four Rorschach judges failed to conclude that he had schizophrenia. Instead he was variously described as having a 'compulsive character', an 'inadequate character', and an obsessional personality. The fifth was suffering from a neurotic disorder but was diagnosed by no fewer than eleven of the judges as being psychotic. Research work of the character briefly described here has led many psychologists to the conclusion that projective tests are misleading. In all, projective test interpretations are an unfortunate example of interprofessional collaboration which led to a sorry outcome.

Therapy

We now return to the general theme of the collaboration between the two disciplines. It could not be expected that psychologists, rarely with less than five years and often with more than eight years of university study, would be content for long with 'test-bashing'. By the early 1960s they were showing an enthusiastic and active interest in therapy. For many of them, especially in the United States, therapy meant psychotherapy, and psychotherapy meant Freudian-based interpretive therapy. Although the evidence on the therapeutic effects of interpretive treatment is unsatisfactory,[4] psychologists are conducting this form of therapy in increasing numbers, to the discomfort of some members of the psychiatric profession, who give the impression that they are in favour of restrictive practices. Meanwhile an alternative approach to treatment and rehabilitation, called behaviour modification or behaviour therapy, was developed, largely by psychologists. These procedures are now beginning to make an effective contribution. Many of the psychologists who helped to establish the alternative methods were recruits from psychological laboratories and their approach was distinguished by a concern for experimental controls, measurement, validation and replicability. An important consequence of this work was the early recognition that what is now referred to as the 'medical model' of psychiatric disorders is deficient (see below, p. 151). Before turning to a consideration of this theoretical advance, it is worth pointing out some of the practical contributions of psychology to psychiatry.

Psychologists introduced some assessment techniques which can help in diagnosis and the evalution of treatment. These methods range from standardised psychometric procedures such as intelligence tests, aptitude tests and personality inventories to the less creditable tests of brain damage and the misleading projective tests. They also include the increasingly useful behavioural assessment and observation techniques, improved rating scales and conceptual tests. An array of psychophysiological measures, which promised sophistication and objectivity, were also developed but unfortunately they are still beset by serious technical snags.

Psychologists were also responsible for introducing news forms of psychotherapy, perhaps the most notable being the non-directive method of Carl Rogers.[5] He postulated that there are three necessary and sufficient conditions for effective therapy. It was argued that constructive personality change (the suggested purpose of therapy) is facilitated when the therapist is 'warm, empathic and genuine'. He added that when these conditions are present in large measure the resulting improvement will be more striking; however, if any one of these conditions is not present, constructive change will not take place. This approach to psychotherapy has many attractive features, not least of which is the admirable clarity with which Rogers presents his views. They generated a considerable amount of research and, in brief, it has been found that although the three therapeutic conditions described by Rogers may be facilitative, they are not necessary.[4] A particularly challenging aspect of Rogers's theory was his assertion that academic knowledge and training are irrelevant to the practice of effective psychotherapy; any person, irrespective of his training or knowledge, who relates to people in a warm, empathic and genuine manner can be a successful therapist. Although this issue is far from settled, there are signs that Rogers may be correct.

The practice of non-directive therapy has also drawn attention to the operation of powerful non-specific factors which make a beneficial contribution to the various types of psychotherapy—and indeed, to the operation of placebo responses (see Chapter 6).

Psychologists made a specific contribution to our understanding of neurosis by helping to identify the occurrence of a high rate of spontaneous improvement among patients with neurotic problems. In a crude early estimate, Professor Eysenck suggested that as many as two-thirds of all neurotic patients improve substantially within a two-year period. Although comprehensive figures are still not available, this estimate is not far off the mark.[5] In addition to the intrinsic importance of the observation that the majority of neurotic patients improve within a comparatively short period, recognition of this high rate of spontaneous improvement cast a new light on claims made by psychotherapists. It was seen that their claims of success rarely exceeded the spontaneous recovery rate, and on occasions fell below it.

Dissatisfaction with the evidence on the effects of various forms of psychotherapy prompted a search for new methods of dealing with behavioural and other problems. One of the most promising of these new departures, behaviour modification, consists of a number of techniques which include desensitisation, flooding, modelling, aversion therapy and operant conditioning. The first three are used for the reduction of fear and anxiety states, aversion therapy is used to suppress unwanted behaviour, and operant conditioning has a wide range of applications—mostly designed to establish more adaptive behaviour. This conditioning method has so far been most successfully applied to the training of intellectually handicapped children and adults (see Chapter 1).

Desensitisation was developed by Professor Wolpe for the treatment of neurotic disorders in which anxiety is a central element. It has been used extensively in the treatment of neurotic patients, and the procedure and its rationale have been the subject of numerous experimental investigations.[6] The technique involves the gradual and graduated presentation of anxiety-evoking images while the patient is deeply relaxed. The patient acquires the ability to tolerate these fear-evoking images and this improvement usually transfers to the real-life situation. Much of our

144

knowledge about fears and how to reduce them has been obtained from the study of normal people who show an excessive fear of spiders, snakes, worms and the like. As might be anticipated, it is easier to reduce the fears of normal people than those who have more serious and broader disturbances. Nevertheless, desensitisation has proved to be sufficiently robust for successful use in psychiatry. The present state of the experimental and clinical evidence on desensitisation can be summarised in this way. Therapy based on desensitisation effectively reduces phobic behaviour. It is unnecessary to ascertain the origin of a phobia in order to eliminate it, nor is it necessary to change the person's attitudes or to modify his personality. The elimination of a phobia is rarely followed by a new problem or symptom. The effects of desensitisation are potentiated by 'real-life' practice and, where practicable, 'real-life' desensitisation is preferable to imaginal forms.

A recent off-shoot of the desensitisation technique is one in which the patient is exposed to the fear-provoking situation with relatively little preparation. This type of treatment is called flooding, and has achieved some promising early successes, particularly in the management of neurotic disorders, especially phobias and obsessive problems. A third procedure which has yielded exceptionally good laboratory results so far is called modelling. This form of treatment derives from the fact that when a fearful person observes someone else acting in a comparatively fearless manner, preferably on many occasions, it will tend to reduce the observer's own fears. In some respect it can be thought of as overcoming fear by imitating a model who can cope relatively boldly in the relevant situation. The therapeutic effect of this type of modelling is greatly enhanced when the person who is afraid follows through his observation of the successful model by copying the model's conduct. This variation is called modelling with participation. The clinical value of modelling has yet to be determined but it seems probable that it will be put to greatest effect in preventing and overcoming childhood fears.

The clinical effectiveness of the fear-reducing techniques of behaviour therapy is attested to by two types of evidence; individual case-histories[7] and controlled clinical trials.[8]

Aversion therapy is used predominantly for the treatment of behaviour disorders in which the patient's conduct is undesirable but self-rewarding (such as alcoholism and sexual disorders). The treatment is designed to bring about a strong connection between the undesirable behaviour and some unpleasant experience (for example, whisky and acute nausea) or to make the unpleasantness a consequence of the undesirable behaviour. It is hoped that by repeatedly associating the undesirable behaviour with some unpleasantness, such behaviour will ultimately cease. Because of the pleasure which most of the disorders usually treated by this form of technique are capable of producing, it is often necessary and desirable to introduce alternative forms of satisfaction for the patient concerned. So, in the case of a person suffering from bizarre sexual fetishism, the aim of treatment would be to suppress the undesirable behaviour and encourage more acceptable and satisfying forms of sexual activity. Although aversion therapy is rated by most patients as being less unpleasant than a visit to the dentist, it has aroused a certain amount of controversy. The majority opinion seems to be that as it involves the administration of unpleasant stimulation, no patient should be offered the treatment as a first choice; and it should certainly not be given except with the informed consent of the patient. The clinical effectiveness of aversion therapy has not yet been determined with accuracy, but it seems to be effective in the treatment of certain kinds of sexual disorder and moderately effective in the treatment of alcoholism.[9]

Operant conditioning treatment techniques are derived from the research reported by Skinner, and their particular strength is that they enable one to generate and shape new kinds of behaviour. Roughly speaking, this is achieved by rewarding effective and appropriate behaviour and by withholding rewards after inappropriate and ineffective behaviour. The constructive power of these procedures has been of great value in the management of behaviour problems which arise because a person has for one reason or another failed to acquire appropriate behaviour. So, for example, it has had considerable success in helping to train retarded people to care for themselves, feed themselves, avoid soiling and wetting themselves, engaging in more easily understood communication and so on (see Chapter 11). It has also been applied with a slight measure of success in the training or retraining of speech-deficient children.

The full clinical value of behaviour modification methods is still under assessment; discussions of recent progress can be found in the works of Marks,[10] Meyer and Chesser,[11] Rachman[4] and Franks[12] among others. In a recently published special report, *Behaviour Therapy and Psychiatry,* the American Psychiatric Association concluded that behaviour therapy procedures 'now unquestionably have much to offer informed clinicians in the service of modern clinical and social psychiatry'. It is now an accepted form of treatment, and the British and American psychiatric associations,

147

among others, consider that it is necessary for psychiatric trainees to receive instruction in the subject.

Taking the long view, an important contribution of the psychologists to psychiatry was their introduction of improved methodology and heightened critical standards. They also made a useful contribution to our understanding of certain types of psychological abnormality, especially those of a neurotic type and most notably phobias and compulsions. However, their major theoretical contribution may prove to be their successful criticisms of the undiscriminating and hence misleading application of the medical model to problems of abnormal behaviour.

Psychiatry's contribution

The contributions of psychiatrists to psychology have been of a different kind and can be grouped in three categories: the provision of facilities, introduction to clinical methods and material, and education in patient care. Psychiatry was the first medical speciality to promote psychological work. Positions were created for psychologists and they received support and encouragement from their psychiatric colleagues who, earlier than other medical personnel, had the prescience to recognise the importance of psychological factors in their work. Many psychiatrists invited their new colleagues to enter the front line of daily practice and the effect of this was to promote the growth of a socially conscious group of applied scientists skilled in helping people in psychological distress. In this way a bridge was built from the often remote psychological laboratories, furnished with memory drums and small animals, to clinics crowded with unhappy and handicapped people.

The clinical applications of psychology helped to provide a more human aspect to the science. In earlier years students who entered psychology eager to gain an improved understanding of their own and other people's behaviour were sometimes bewildered and disappointed by the discovery that psychological texts devoted most of their space to extensive descriptions of rodent behaviour, lightened by references to trivialities of human behaviour. In this setting, the challenge offered by psychiatrists of grappling with the intellectual and practical problems of abnormal human behaviour was welcome and refreshing.

Although psychiatry and psychiatrists benefited by the arrival of clinical psychologists, there was a price to be paid. They sometimes had to suffer psychologists who displayed a superior scientific understanding and even affected a superior morality. In the United States, the phenomenal growth of clinical psychology led to a situation in which psychiatry often lost in the competition for funds. Interprofessional disagreements arose in delineating the borders between the two professions, particularly in the practice of psychotherapy, and American psychiatrists fought a losing and needless battle to obtain the exclusive right to therapeutic services. Elsewhere, as in many parts of Europe, the battle has not yet been joined. Although the demand for psychiatric services so far exceeds the supply that no psychiatrist is in danger of joining the dole queue, they feel understandably pressed by the rapid multiplication of psychologists. To make matters worse, the psychologists are rarely grateful and indeed are too often resentful.

The collaboration with psychiatry also gives rise to some difficulties for psychologists. Even when their skill, training and experience are superior to those of their colleagues in psychiatry, psychologists are almost always subordinate. They may find themselves being patronised. Final 'clinical responsibility' (rarely defined) almost always rests with the psychiatrist, be he senior or junior. So for example, psychiatric registrars in their first year of training are in a position to interfere with the work of the most experienced of clinical psychologists, who might have as many as thirty years' or more experience behind him. Again, the status and salary of a psychiatrist are almost always higher than those of his counterpart in psychology. The difference was explained by an American psychologist: 'What is the difference between a psychiatrist and a psychologist? Thirty thousand dollars a year.'

On the scientific side, the medical approach of psychiatrists sometimes has the effect of inhibiting or distorting psychological thinking and practice. The excessive use of intelligence tests, for example, was partly the result of pressures from psychiatrists for this type of reassurance. A vast amount of psychologists' time was wasted—time which could have been devoted to research and to the care and comfort of distressed people. More important, however, was the way in which psychologists, exposed to the medical model of abnormal behaviour, accepted it uncritically for over thirty years. This unfortunate influence was an obstacle to scientific advance.

A last example of the undesirable effects of an over-zealous use of the medical approach can be seen in respect of homosexuality. In less than twenty-five years it has undergone three major transformations. First it was a crime, then it became a psychiatric *symptom* and now it is being seen as an acceptable expression of sexual diversity, no longer abnormal.

Psychiatric psychology

What is the medical model?

It is no easy task to explain the weaknesses of the medical model because there is no single agreed version of what the model looks like. In our view, the medical model of abnormal behaviour includes some combination of the following features. First and foremost, it is assumed that most forms of abnormal behaviour fall within the scope of medical knowledge and practice. Psychological problems or problems of abnormal behaviour are regarded as being analogous to physical abnormalities. Many types of abnormal behaviour, from hallucinations to truancy, from stuttering to repeated drunkenness, and from extreme shyness to premature ejaculation, are considered to be manifestations, that is, symptoms, of illness. Hallucinations are frequently interpreted as a symptom of psychotic illness (insanity), excessive shyness often is taken as an indication of neurotic illness, and so on.

The illnesses inferred from the occurrence of abnormal behaviour, regarded as symptoms, are generally construed as having an inner cause. The cause is often assumed to be physical in nature; specifically, an infection, injury or systemic dysfunction. Although the psychoanalytic theory of mental illnesses is more complex, it shares the major assumption of an inner etiology which gives rise to symptoms. In place of physical causes of illness, Freud made the important substitution of complex psychological causes (for instance an unresolved Oedipus complex) but he continued to theorise within a medical model.

The state of illness denoted by abnormal behaviour is regarded as being different from and discontinuous with a healthy state (characterised by normal behaviour). In illness, it is assumed that either one's

151

judgement or control, if not both, are impaired. The illness is assumed to have a distinct etiology and to run a determined course; it has a prognosis.

The appearance of symptoms, in mental illness the appearance of abnormal behaviour, requires classification and diagnosis. The main diagnostic groups are: neurosis, psychosis, personality disorder. Once a diagnosis is made, forms of treatment and care are advised or administered (by doctors, in hospitals or clinics). There is an emphasis on physical forms of treatment and, as in physical illnesses, this often comes down to the prescription of drugs.

It is assumed that the process from diagnosis to treatment and after-care should be controlled and largely conducted by medical personnel. Hence, to return to our earlier examples, excessive shyness or premature ejaculation or stuttering are seen as medical problems— requiring diagnosis and treatment. Another important aspect of the medical model is the assumption that a mental illness, having an underlying cause, is best dealt with by treating this *underlying* cause. Tackling the symptoms, that is the abnormal behaviour itself, is at best superficial. Even when the abnormal behaviour is successfully modified, the substitution of another manifestation of the underlying cause can be expected —a substitute symptom in fact. The medical model virtually precludes attempts to modify abnormal behaviour in a direct manner.

For a long while the medical view of abnormal behaviour as illness went unchallenged, partly no doubt because it is an appropriate model for some types of disorder. Some of them fit comfortably into a medical schema. For example, paresis is a syphilitic infection which damages the brain and results in abnormal behaviour, including delusions, impaired memory and so on. Similarly, Korsakoff's syndrome, a disorder resulting from prolonged abuse of alcohol, is characterised by abnormal experiences, confusion, impaired memory and sensory disturbances.

Psychologists followed their psychiatric colleagues in over-generalising from examples such as paresis to a wide variety of disorders in which abnormal behaviour or experiences are an important feature. So a person with excessive fears was considered to be neurotically ill, a man who stole repetitively was said to suffer from a psychopathic illness, a woman who was persistently unhappy was diagnosed as having a depressive illness, a man who could not maintain friendships was suffering from interpersonal problems indicative of a personality disorder. The view that abnormal behaviour is a medical problem gained such wide acceptance that nowadays psychiatrists accept patients suffering from such diverse problems as homosexuality, excessive drinking, impotence, marital unhappiness, reading retardation, delusions, stuttering, occupational inadequacy, bed-wetting, compulsive handwashing, delayed speech, inability to use public transport, exhibitionism, social isolation and many others.

Without labouring the point by examining each of these examples in turn, it is apparent that many of them (for instance, fear of transport, marital difficulties, occupational inadequacy) are unlikely to be the symptoms of an illness in the senses described earlier. There is no clear division between these problems and others of ordinary living; there is little cause for assuming an underlying pathology. And, of course, it is rare to find a physical basis for problems of this kind, or a single cause or an inner cause. Almost always, an analysis of the problem reveals several contributing factors, present and past. One is obliged to consider the person's earlier experiences, present social and occupational circumstances, recent stressful events and other factors, and then use them to build up an explanation which attaches different emphases to the many variables involved and to the way in which they have combined to produce the behaviour which is constituting a problem. One assembles a psychological model incorporating many factors.

Searches for an underlying cause, physical or mental, and an exclusive reliance on physical methods of treatment are seldom successful. If bed-wetting, compulsive handwashing, stuttering, exhibitionism, excessive drinking and many other examples, are approached as illnesses, then productive and sensible formulations might be precluded. It is not clear why these problems should be regarded as falling within the province of medicine and there is even less cause for considering them to be psychiatric problems. Indeed, even if they were illnesses or signs of illness, there is little in the syllabus of medical colleges to prepare a practitioner who is called upon to analyse or modify them. Courses in psychology and particularly those dealing with abnormal behaviour would be more pertinent. In recognition of this point of view, many medical schools are now placing greater emphasis on psychological and other behavioural sciences.

Returning to the major argument, many psychologists and increasing numbers of psychiatrists now feel that the medical view of abnormal behaviour and experiences was unduly stretched from those instances where it is appropriate, to cover an impossibly large and diverse group of problems. Apart from the psychotic disorders (mainly schizophrenia), autism, paresis and those disorders caused by injury, growths or infections, there are not many contemporary psychiatric problems which qualify unquestionably for the label of 'illness'.

We should also point out that it is no longer unanimously agreed that schizophrenia is a form of mental illness. There are critics today, especially in the United States, who prefer to regard the constellation of abnormal behaviour and experiences called schizophrenia as being unusual but not pathological. Certainly it is still not possible to demonstrate either that the cause of schizophrenia is physical, or that there is any one underlying cause. It is also known that the diagnosis of schizophrenia is more widely and freely used in the United States than in Europe; certain 'American types' of schizophrenia would not be so diagnosed in Britain.[13] These two points are common targets of the critics who also remark on the acknowledged fact that the families of schizophrenic patients are on average more disturbed than other families. Despite these problems there are reasons for retaining the view that schizophrenia, at least as recognised in Europe, is a form of illness.[14] There is strong evidence of a major genetic contribution to schizophrenia, it does follow expected courses, it has a typical age of onset and it does carry a reasonably clear prognosis. The affected person's judgement and control commonly are impaired and his behaviour is usually discontinuous with normal forms in some important respects.

Even more difficult problems of distinction arise in consideration of persistent unhappiness. When does it qualify for the clinical label of 'depression'? And is depression an abnormal experience, or an illness, or both? In practice, the clinical label is generally applied to people who suffer from intense and prolonged unhappiness. The dividing line is rough and hence awkward to use, especially in borderline cases. However, there is a plausible case for subdividing depression into two main types. If further research produces the hoped-for biological (probably biochemical) distinction between the two postulated types of depression, it will help to clarify the debate about whether and when persistent, severe unhappiness can reasonably be considered to be a form of illness. It is also worth recalling that until relatively recent times, persistent unhappiness was *not* considered to be a form of illness; instead, such people were merely described as being melancholic.

The differences between mental illnesses and behavioural problems are not always straightforward. There are instances where 'mental illness' is indubitably the correct way to construe the problem and other examples where the term 'illness' is inappropriate. It is necessary to find a clear path between these two extreme points of view by careful analysis of each example.

The most promising basis for distinctions is probably that of dysfunction instead of damage, but we are immediately confronted with the intricate and difficult problems of defining psychiatric dysfunction.

Is the distinction between 'illness' behaviour and other types of abnormal behaviour a mere quibble? In view of the practical and scientific implications of such a distinction, we feel that despite the complexities involved it is more than verbal exercise. The label given to a person with psychological difficulties can of course have a significant effect on the way in which he views himself. When we describe a person's difficulties as being a manifestation of illness, it is usually assumed that his responsibility for his own conduct is impaired; the problems are regarded as being largely beyond his control. This approach encourages passivity. 'If I am ill,' the argument goes, 'then cure me.' And we might add, in passing, that cures are usually expected to arrive in the shape of pills. Many of the people who reject the medical model of psychological problems have significantly substituted the word 'client' in place of 'patient'.

If we approach a person's psychological difficulties as problems of behaviour and experience, avoiding any suggestion of illness, he is more likely to retain a feeling of responsibility and to participate actively in the development of satisfactory alternatives. An exhibitionist who is given a medical diagnosis, informing him that he is ill, may be less willing to cooperate actively in carrying out a programme designed to stimulate satisfactory sexual alternatives and improved self-control. He believes that publicly displaying his genitals is the symptom of an illness and hence is more likely to ask for pills, or even for an operation.

If one develops the argument that many of the personal difficulties currently regarded as signs of illness are in fact better seen as problems of behaviour, it becomes necessary to consider *where* and *by whom* assistance should be arranged. As the people in difficulty are not patients in the ordinary sense and are not in need of *treatment,* it might be preferable for them to attend advisory or guidance agents of some description. As a matter of fact, this is the course taken by most people. Reviewing a number of surveys and other investigations, Bergin pointed out that 'the majority of people who experience psychological disturbance do *not* seek out mental health professionals for treatment. Many of them seek counsel, advice and support from a variety of helping persons' including friends, teachers, clergymen, and lawyers.[15] In one of the surveys, it was also found that respondents expressed greater satisfaction with the help they had received from people other than psychiatrists or psychologists. This finding calls to mind the startling observation made by Professor Jerome Frank in 1968, that in the United States more people are treated by religious healers and chiropractors than by psychiatrists and psychologists combined.[16] If our argument has merit, then plans and actions based on the distinction between illness and personal problems will be more rational and more effective than contemporary psychiatric or psychological services—and perhaps also more effective than religious healing, based as it is on an illness model of a different type. Prayers and prescriptions would be replaced by behavioural analyses, counselling, relearning and environmental modifications.

At a psychological centre the person in difficulty would consult specialists in behaviour, people who have been trained in psychology and behaviour modification, with or without a background of medical training. Naturally, people suffering from mental illness would remain in the care of psychiatrists; medical personnel interested in behavioural problems could readily acquire the necessary skills and, as mentioned earlier, medical schools are now devoting much more attention to psychological topics. Medical students of the future can be expected to spend less time studying Henry Gray on anatomy and more time reading Jeffrey Gray on fear.

Attempts to provide guidance of the type we are advocating should be preceded by an analysis of the abnormal behaviour or experiences, or both, and the findings then used in designing a programme of behaviour modification. The aim of these programmes is not the achievement of a 'cure'; instead they are intended to help the person to develop more adaptive behaviour and to reduce unadaptive and distressing behaviour or experiences. In many instances there is no need to construe the problem in terms of illness; it would be misleading to speak of 'treatment' and impossible to 'cure' anything.

Psychological problems need psychological solutions. If it appears that an over-protected young man's compulsive handwashing arose out of a steadily growing fear of germs and that the fear was being maintained by the temporary relief obtained from handwashing and by excessive parental concern, several steps might be considered. The parental behaviour and attitudes might be modified by direct guidance and example. The man's fear of germs might be reduced by desensitising him. Attempts could also be made to encourage increasingly independent behaviour, including perhaps a move from home.

In this example, easily multiplied, it can be seen that little is gained by calling the man ill (which he probably is not) and no single or physical underlying cause is assumed. The problem behaviour is analysed, several putative contributing factors are identified and a programme of modification is designed. It can be seen that a medical approach to this example of abnormal compulsive behaviour is not the only model available. When it assumes a false identity between compulsive problems and the illnesses typified by problems such as paresis, the medical view can be misleading. If it were strictly adhered to, it would rule out attempts to deal with the problem behaviour directly. In the present example, direct attempts to reduce the frequency and duration of handwashing would be inadvisable. For a considerable time, in fact, people suffering from this type of difficulty were advised, as were their relatives, to avoid restricting the excessive washing. The elimination of the symptom of handwashing, it was argued, was certain to be followed by the appearance of a new and possibly more serious symptom or illness. Despite this view and the

159

advice given, attempts were made at direct modification of excessive handwashing. Recent research has shown that even when direct modification is successful new symptoms or difficulties rarely arise.[10, 17]

Sanity and insanity

The distinction between the mental illness model and the psychological approach is also of considerable professional significance. Problems which are manifestations of mental illness should, without argument, remain the responsibility primarily of psychiatrists; naturally, other types of personal problems need not fall within the competence of psychiatrists. In 1973, a Working Party of the Royal College of Psychiatrists submitted a Memorandum to the Department of Health expressing their views on the role of the psychological services in the Health Service.[18] Despite the inflexibly conservative opinions stated in that Memorandum, the Council of the Royal College accepted it. Although numbers of British psychiatrists have since expressed their strong disagreement with this document of the Royal College, at the time of writing it remains the official view of the profession. The Memorandum rejects all criticisms of the mental illness model:

> It is recognised that there is a school of thought which denies the concept of mental illness and considers that the symptoms hitherto classified as mental illness, mental disorder, neurosis, psychosis, personality disorder etc., should be regarded as psychological behavioural maladjustments and should be treated outside the medical ambit. These views are not acceptable to the College.

Among a host of weaknesses which will ensure its early relegation to the archives, the Memorandum

160

tion of Rosenhan's study would produce less disturbing results.

Care and cure

It has been observed that we place greater emphasis on cure than on care. More time, effort and attention are devoted to patients with circumscribed, remediable illnesses than to those suffering from chronic problems or handicaps. People suffering from chronic problems, especially those handicapped by severe intellectual retardation, have traditionally been near the bottom of all lists of priority. The undue emphasis on cures is evident also in psychiatric practices and has been absorbed by psychologists. Recognition of the distinction between behavioural problems and mental illnesses might have the useful result of redistributing medical, psychological and social efforts, thereby improving the balance between cure and care. It may also assist in replacing the idea that there are only two possibilities—treatment or no help. This view is illustrated by the phrase: 'Sorry, there is no treatment for your problem; we can't help you.'

As clinical psychologists expand their interests to include other branches of medicine and health services, what course will psychiatric psychology take? As the process of expansion is likely to be slow, the majority of clinical psychologists will continue to concern themselves with abnormalities of behaviour for a considerable time to come. There will be no shortage of work. The provision of services for people with psychological difficulties or mental illnesses, or both, will require many hands. Fruitful collaboration between psychology and psychiatry will certainly continue. Regrettably, interdisciplinary bickering will also continue. On the scientific

163

side, it is reasonable to anticipate improved understanding of abnormal experiences, the adoption of more satisfactory models of abnormal behaviour and of mental illness, improved techniques of assessment, and we can expect advances in the power and applicability of behaviour modification procedures. Psychotherapy (of various types) will be practised for some time to come, irrespective of its scientific standing. We can however look forward to a more realistic appraisal of its uses and limitations. Even if psychotherapy fails to alter problem behaviour, people are likely to offer and receive it—because many unhappy people find that talking to a sympathetic listener is comforting.

been well informed and expressed moderate anticipatory fear had a more comfortable and less emotional period of convalescence.

These findings, although sparse, appear to suggest that a moderate amount of anticipatory fear about realistic stress provides a useful form of inoculation. Research work of a more general kind reported by Lazarus and his colleagues in the University of California supports this idea.[2] Over a period of many years they have been investigating the effects of stress and possible means of reducing the emotional disruption produced by events of this kind. Broadly speaking, they have found that various forms of rehearsal, including mental rehearsal, serve to reduce the disturbance caused by the stressful events. It seems that rehearsals achieve their effects by reducing at least two of the major determinants of fear and anxiety—novelty and suddenness.[3]

Lazarus emphasises the importance of having a strategy for coping with stress and, clearly, appropriate rehearsals will stimulate the successful search for adequate means of coping with the real stress when it does occur.[2] Viewed against the background of this type of research on stress and its psychological effects, the potential value of psychological preparation for hospital admissions, surgery and other painful and uncomfortable treatments seems assured.

The experiment carried out by Egbert and his colleagues on ninety-seven adult surgical patients provides some practical encouragement for this type of approach.[4] The patients were admitted to hospital for abdominal operations and assigned at random to one of two groups, which were, of course, equated on all important factors. Before the operation the patients in the first group had a visit from one of the surgical team who gave them information about the operation and its effects. They

167

were told how long the operation would last, where and when they would regain consciousness, the location and intensity of the expected post-operative pain, assurances about analgesic medication and so on. The patients in the second group did not receive any of the preparatory information.

In the five days after the operation, patients in the first group required only half as much sedation as did the patients in the group who had received no special preparations. The informed group also needed considerably less morphine. As might be expected from the research mentioned earlier, the poorly informed patients experienced more emotional disturbance in the post-operative period. A particularly interesting finding is that although the medical and surgical teams were unaware of the group identity of any of the patients, those who had received preparatory information showed quicker improvement, as a group, than did the poorly informed patients. On average, the informed patients were discharged three days earlier than the others. These interesting findings make it plain that we need a great deal more information about the psychological effects of hospital admissions, treatment, surgery and the like. It should be equally obvious that this entire subject is fascinating and potentially valuable. In our opinion, patients will benefit considerably from determined and systematic attempts to provide psychological preparation for their admission to hospital and treatment. This should include, at least, full factual information, emotional reassurance and some inoculation. We look forward to the day when greater medical and nursing attention is given to the patient's need for emotional comfort and reassurance and less attention to the vagaries of his bowel movements.

tion, even if temporary, was likely to produce irreversible and serious damage to his personality, frequently culminating in prolonged anti-social behaviour. These alarmist views have been placed in proper perspective in recent years,[8, 9] but the recommendations which they prompted were humane and sometimes effective. The unfortunate consequence, however, was that many parents and doctors became excessively reluctant to admit children to hospital and felt needlessly guilty if they did so.

In examining the effects of admission to hospital, it is useful to separate the immediate and short-term consequences from the long-term effects which might be expected, say, several months after discharge. Although this elementary distinction is of some value, unfortunately it does not overcome some of the other confounding problems encountered in work of this kind. For example, how can we distinguish between the distress caused by admission to hospital and that caused by the illness itself; between the effects of the illness and the medical procedures such as injections, drips, operations and the rest; or between the effects of admission to a *hospital* from the distress which might be caused by a separation from the child's parents? Despite the considerable methodological problems, enough information has now been collected to permit some tentative conclusions.

The undesirable effects of prolonged separation, exemplified by long-term institutional care, were sometimes quoted as an argument against hospital admission. An accumulation of information on the effects of short hospital stays (which is of course easier to obtain than data on institutional effects) has now led to a more balanced view.

It appears that the unfamiliarity of the hospital, the

171

staff and the routine is a major cause of psychological upset. After the initial period of disturbance, most children grow accustomed to the change and their distress decreases within a few days. Very few show any lasting signs of distress after they have returned home. Children between the ages of seven months and four years are the ones most likely to suffer substantial distress—a finding compatible with other evidence that this is a period during which children are particularly likely to be upset by separation.[8] It appears that well-adjusted children with satisfactory parental relationships cope well with the stresses of hospital. Adverse reactions of a long-term character are rarely encountered in children of this type. Preparation for admission can reduce the expected disturbance.

Evidence? —

There is evidence of moderate but widespread upset and anxiety in parents when their children are admitted and some indications that these emotional reactions provoke similar responses in the children themselves. Thus the children of very anxious parents are likely to be more distressed in hospital.

Evidence of the effects of maternal separation on young children is consistent with these findings and indeed, the separation of the child from his mother (and father) may well be responsible for much of the upset experienced on entering hospital. Yarrow[9] and Rutter[8] have given lucid accounts of the subject of maternal deprivation and placed the matter in its correct perspective. Broadly speaking, temporary breaks in the child's important affectional bonds are seen to produce distress but rarely any long-term consequences—unless the affectional bonds are unsatisfactory before the separation. Long-term disruptions of affectional bonds in young children can, however, have far more serious and enduring adverse consequences. We also need to

172

bear in mind that satisfactory parents, not doctors, nurses or psychologists, are the most effective people for reducing a child's anxiety, pain and other forms of distress.

For reasons of this type, and others not mentioned, the Platt Committee recommended that admission to hospital should be confined to those cases in which it is unavoidable. Similarly, they recommended the establishment of mother-and-child units, which would of course be of particular value in these cases. By admitting the mother with the child, a double purpose might be served. In the first place, it would avoid disrupting the mother–child bond and, secondly, the mother would be present and available at precisely that period of the child's life when he most needs care, comfort and affectionate attention. The Committee also recommended that parents should be given unrestricted visiting access to their children in hospital.

Recently, Stacey and her colleagues set out to study the implementation of certain parts of the report in two selected hospitals.[10] They attempted to assess the extent, depth, duration and individual variations in the disturbance of children admitted to these two hospitals. The main weakness of an otherwise valuable study is the absence of psychological data or expertise. They obtained information about ninety-five children, all under the age of five, who were admitted for tonsillectomy. Two-thirds of the children had received some preparation for their admission to hospital but of course it was less common among the emergency admissions. They found poor arrangements for the reception of the child and parents. But the most common complaint of the parents was, once again, the inadequacy of the information provided by the hospital staff. One-third of the parents in the sample made this specific complaint and it was found that nurses were regarded as the least satisfactory source of information. Less than half of the mothers found that the official policy of unrestricted visiting of children under the age of five was actually in operation; one-fifth of the mothers said that they were allowed less than one hour a day with their children.

Stacey and her colleagues relate these deficiencies to the conception which nurses and doctors have of their role.[10] According to Stacey, nurses do not feel that their role 'includes playing with or talking to the children on the ward' [p. 110]. They felt that their duties were to wash, dress and serve the children with food. They had almost no contact with the children outside these nursing routines. While most nurses accepted parents on the ward, almost all of them were opposed to unrestricted visiting. It was found that this attitude was translated into behaviour which defeated the official policy of unrestricted visiting. Prolonged or frequent parental visits were plainly discouraged. The message was received; most parents said that they were concerned to avoid 'being in the way'—again, 'they expect the nurses to be busy . . . and overworked' [*op. cit.*, p. 115]. The nurses had little contact with the parents and were observed to disappear when the parents arrived. There was little provision, physical or social, for parental help, let alone visits. These acts of omission served to discourage parents from visiting, of course.

The authors offer some tentative views on the characteristics of vulnerable children. They suggest that the children who are most likely to experience undue disturbance are uncommunicative, isolated, shy, very young or only children. Also in this category are children who have recently been separated from their parents or who have over-anxious parents.

Stacey and her co-authors end with many sensible

suggestions, endorsing the Platt recommendations and adding their own. They urge that occupation should be provided for the children during the day (for instance, by play-group leaders or nursery teachers) as it was found that the majority of children spent an astonishing amount of time entirely on their own during each day. They also recommend the removal of the physical, personal and professional barriers to parental visits. They would like to see hospital staffs encouraging parents to participate actively in caring for their children, a move which would of course require that space and equipment of a suitable kind was provided (such as feeding-chairs, toys, bathrooms and TV seats). They further recommend improved preparation and health education both at home and in schools and a form of induction process for children about to go into hospital. All their proposals seem to us to be both desirable and sensible without being over-elaborate. They have the great merit of being open to proper psychological, and other, evaluation. To their suggestions we would like to add the following:

1   Attempt to reduce the vulnerability of children by arranging for parental action, school action and efforts by the local health authorities. For example, it should be possible to show films and video-tapes at school of children being prepared for hospital and coping with the routines in a hospital. Also, parents could be encouraged to make arrangements for their children to sleep away from home on suitable occasions at a younger age than is perhaps customary.
2   Knowledge about the value of modelling for teaching children how to cope could be used in hospitals by using a system of peer models.[11] Each new admission could be assigned to a 'veteran' patient who would be

asked to guide him through his first hours and through the standard routines required.

3 Direct preparations could be given to children who know that they are to go into hospital. For example, they could be shown preparatory films, make visits to the ward before admission, practise some of the routines in the hospital setting and so on.

4 Parents could be told how they can be most effective during the child's period in hospital and, again, it should be possible to use film and real models in transmitting the knowledge and skill. The parents could be taught to cope with their own anxieties and how to reduce the anxiety and distress of their children.

5 Nurses and doctors working with children could be taught about the psychology of separations, illnesses and admissions, and trained to comfort children and encourage the active help of parents. None of these efforts will qualify as successful until the last nurse is heard to explain that she 'cannot talk to the children because she has too much work to do'.

All these ideas and proposals are unnecessarily elaborate and time-consuming—if our health services are for ever to be seen as physically based and oriented. When broader and more compassionate views prevail, the psychological impact of what we do with and for our patients will assume its proper importance.

The value of each of the specific proposals will need to be assessed by the appropriate research investigations. There is some evidence, but by no means sufficient in quantity or quality, to support the *general* idea that preparation for the experiences of an admission to hospital is of value. In an often quoted study by Prugh and others the value of psychological preparation for admission and the explicit provision of emotional support during the hospital period seemed to be demonstrated in a series of 100 children.[12] These children apparently showed less fear, unhappiness and emotional upset during their stay in hospital than did a comparable 100 children who received neither the psychological preparation nor the emotional support. For a variety of technical reasons, the experimental design used in this study was faulty and consequently the conclusions must be tentative. Unfortunately, the weaknesses in this study, which included a confusing mixture of procedures, the absence of 'blind' assessors and other deficiencies, are also present in the few other studies carried out during this period. A more satisfactory study was reported by a group working at the Yale School of Nursing.[13] In this investigation the children in the experimental group (and their parents) were given information about hospital procedures and a full account of what the child might expect before and after the completion of the operation to remove their tonsils. A comparable group of children in the control condition received normal hospital care, nursing and medical procedures, but were not given preparatory information or advice. The observations and assessments were carefully controlled and the major outcome was that children who received the additional preparation displayed fewer signs of emotional disturbance while in the hospital or during their convalescence at home.

Our limited evidence on the psychological value of preparing adults and children for admission to and treatment in hospital is at least consistent and has the added virtue of being common sense. The sophisticated psychological research on preparing people to cope with various forms of stress is uncommon, but no less sensible for that.[2]

11 Custodians or teachers?

The contribution of psychology to psychiatric care is usually recognised, but the recent and relatively larger contribution of psychology to the care and teaching of intellectually retarded people has yet to be appreciated. The modern tendency for scientific advances to be paraded prematurely has not occurred; to the contrary, the good news has spread slowly. Comparatively few people in education, health and social services seem to be aware of these advances or their practical significance. Nevertheless, sensible and generous planning of assistance can now proceed on the basis of an effective and growing technology. We are in sight of a transition from custodial care to a period of active education and training, during which large numbers of retarded people will be helped to participate in and enjoy more of the normal activities of everyday life.

It is difficult to exaggerate the miseries that exist in many of the custodial institutions. Despite the best intentions and efforts of the staff, many residents live in squalor and degradation which could be alleviated if the staff possessed the available technical knowledge and skill. Travis Thompson has given a vivid account of a visit he made to Faribault State Hospital in 1968, before the introduction of some of these new methods:

I was confronted with sights, sounds and smells which I had never before experienced and hoped that I would never witness again. Seated in the middle of the large ward area

178

shackled to a chair was a young man in his twenties with all of his skin abraded from his knees and blood running down his shins. Along the 70ft wall of the ward were seated approximately fifteen men, huddled in fetal positions, with their heads between their knees. Most of them sat totally still, a few rocked from side to side, a few rocked forward and backward. Beneath half of the chairs were puddles of urine. The room reeked of urine and faeces, and faeces were smeared over the floor, over the arms and legs, and on the trousers and shirts of the numerous residents. Approximately half of the men were partially or totally unclad. Another twenty or so residents were walking, running, or twirling about the room. Some were rapidly twiddling their fingers in front of their faces, others were gnawing at their hands and forearms. Most . . . were scarred . . . the noise level was unbelievable and the ward echoed with hoots, shrieks and wails . . . the two psychiatric technicians who were on duty were continually mopping urine or attending to fights between residents and treating the wounds and abrasions; one patient bit another so forcefully that the wound required medical attention [p. 7].[1]

Before turning to the achievement of Thompson and his colleagues in moving Faribault Hospital from a custodial institution closer to an educational one, it is necessary to describe the background developments that led to the emergence of the technical means for improving institutions of this type. Once in possession of a more optimistic, active approach to the problem it becomes possible to delineate five major aims of work with retarded people: to acquire improved personal skills (e.g. caring for themselves, feeding, clothing, and cleaning themselves daily); to achieve improved recreational skills, bearing in mind that these are seldom seen in custodial institutions; to acquire some occupational skills; to achieve improvements in social competence; to over-

179

come or eliminate the disruptive behaviour which makes them unacceptable outside the institution.

If one regards most of these problems as behavioural deficits, as indeed they are, then one's search turns towards techniques for teaching people more adaptive behaviour. During the past decade a technology for supplying this need has been developing. It is based on the application of operant conditioning theory and techniques, a form of learning which is particularly well suited for use with people who experience difficulty with complex abstract and verbal forms of instruction and education.[2, 3] Operant conditioning enables one to generate new responses and also to improve and strengthen already existing responses which are as yet inadequate. Many of the applications in the field of retardation are based on the simple observation made by Skinner that behaviour is governed by its consequences.[4, 5] In plain terms behaviour that is followed by rewarding consequences will increase in strength, while behaviour that is not followed by rewarding consequences will weaken and decline. Although most psychologists would today agree that Skinner's formulation is an over-simplification and therefore subject to serious limitations, it has fortunately turned out to be the case that *the limits do include the shaping of adequate behaviour* in intellectually retarded people. In justice one should point out that Skinner, who has been so severely criticised for his general system of psychology and its potential applications in society (for instance his recent book *Beyond Freedom and Dignity*), has received little recognition for inspiring by his writings and encouraging by his actions the more effective and humane care of severely retarded people.

The earliest clinical applications of operant conditioning were carried out in the field of adult psychiatry and are best exemplified by the work of Ayllon. With his colleagues he demonstrated the effectiveness of ward training methods in the management and rehabilitation of patients suffering from chronic schizophrenia.[6,7] They were able to shape and improve a range of behaviour patterns in these patients which included the development of appropriate social behaviour, coherent speech and other valuable skills. Moreover they successfully ameliorated a variety of types of disturbed behaviour, such as delusional talk, hoarding, stealing. The results were achieved by the ingenious application of the Skinnerian principles. The techniques have of course been refined and extended during the past decade and are now finding wide application in a large number of psychiatric and other institutions.

In simplified form the application of operant methods consists of six steps. The target behaviour is identified and its frequency is established by baseline recordings. On the basis of these observations the consequences of the behaviour, both desirable and undesirable forms, are analysed. Next, appropriate rewards are selected and these are then explained and introduced to the person. Thereafter, the training proper can begin. Whenever the desirable behaviour occurs, whether spontaneously or by prompting, it is immediately and consistently followed by reward. Every attempt is made to ensure that undesirable behaviour is not followed by a reward. The systematic and patient application of these simple ideas generally results in a strengthening of the desired behaviour and a decline in the undesirable behaviour. Special environmental arrangements need to be made in order to ensure that the newly acquired behaviour is not allowed to be lost.

The application of these methods can be illustrated by reference to a complex case described by Wolf,

Risley and Mees.[8] They have given a vivid account of their successful training of a young autistic boy who was, by all accounts, also severely retarded. Their programme included the development of positive, desirable behaviour as well as the elimination of several forms of undesirable, and even dangerous, behaviour. To begin with they had to cure his very frequent tantrums which, according to their analysis, were being maintained by the immediate and substantial social attention which they produced. They introduced a procedure in which the boy was isolated for a short period whenever the tantrums appeared. This withdrawal of rewards (and the potential for achieving rewards) was soon effective. Once the tantrums had been reduced in frequency, it was possible for Wolf and his colleagues to move on to more positive types of training. The first and most serious problem they faced was to teach the boy to keep on his special spectacles as it was essential that he should wear them in order to save his sight. The difficulties involved in establishing this behaviour in a young, disturbed and almost inaccessible child are all too clear. It proved to be an extremely difficult task, but with patient and careful training they managed to shape the appropriate behaviour, and finally the child wore his glasses on all necessary occasions. Then they attempted to teach the child some acceptable speech. Once again, by providing positive rewards in the form of desired foods and social approval, they had a measure of success. Thereafter they trained him to sleep normally and to eat in a more hygienic and acceptable way.

This successful management of an extremely difficult problem is characteristic of much of the work of the psychologists who participated in the development of these techniques. One of the most admirable aspects of their approach to problems of this type has been their

direction needed to produce total continence' [p. 21]. The main elements of this strategy include the provision of motivation by prompt rewards when deserved, the use of learning by imitation and the shaping up of correct voiding behaviour. At the same time, of course, bad habits such as soiling are discouraged by the consequent need to change and wash one's clothing. In order to ensure that the newly acquired skills are maintained, it is necessary to have trained staff to supervise the residents on and off the ward. The actual training technique is not complicated, but it is arduous. It requires comparatively little apparatus and is applicable to any person who does not have a physical impediment that would prevent him from achieving continence (in practice, very few retarded people have such an impediment). The resident must be able to walk and have normal control of his hands, adequate vision and be capable of understanding simple instructions. To repeat, the intensive training programme consists of a simple cycle of events: the person is given substantial amounts to drink every thirty minutes, is then asked to sit on the toilet for up to twenty minutes, is rewarded for correct urination; returns to the chair and is then rewarded for every five minutes during which his pants stay dry. The cycle is repeated again and again during the course of an eight-hour working day. This is not the place to go into details of the programme, which are fully described by Foxx and Azrin, who also deal candidly with the difficulties that arise. For example, what does one do when the subject goes limp, or when he is generally resistant, or when he has repeated tantrums? Clear guidance on how to deal with problems of this sort is provided. Test trials of this programme carried out by independent investigators are awaited with considerable interest.

187

In the Faribault Hospital project, Bigelow summarised the approach of the group which effected the changes in this way.[10] They focused upon the teaching of specific skills. These were chosen in terms of their practical utility and their relevance to the resident in his normal life. The most relevant types of behaviour were considered to be dressing one's self, eating unassisted, washing one's self and maintaining continence. As a secondary but by no means unimportant aim, they attempted to develop behaviour which would allow the residents to occupy their time satisfactorily, and to amuse themselves. In the design of specific teaching programmes they paid particular attention to the need for each step to be graded and gradual. Working within the tradition established in this style of work, they of course took particular care to ensure that desirable and constructive behaviour was followed promptly and consistently by reward. As always in these programmes, undesirable and disruptive behaviour was reduced by attempting to ensure that it was seldom if ever followed by a reward. Punishment techniques were rarely resorted to and then only in those instances where it was the lesser of two evils—for instance to reduce or stop self-abusive or destructive behaviour, such as to prevent someone from blinding himself as a result of repeatedly banging his head on sharp objects.

Starting with one of the most difficult wards, they first achieved some success with one group of residents, then the next and the next, until what had been a custodial institution gradually became more like a teaching environment, which was the object of their efforts.[1] The changes can be illustrated by one of the worst wards, in which many of the hospital's most difficult patients were accommodated. It included many patients who assaulted each other and also injured themselves. Within a comparatively short period the behaviour of these profoundly retarded, chronically institutionalised patients was considerably improved and they were seen to become more adaptable and to behave more normally for a considerable part of each day. The rate and variety of disruptive behaviour declined in a striking fashion.

When the training programme began on this ward, 65 per cent of the residents were incontinent. After the institution of a specific training programme, the number of incontinent residents shrank to a mere 18 per cent. Or to put it another way, 82 per cent of the residents were capable of keeping themselves clean and dry.

Before the introduction of the modification programme, half the residents either wore no clothing at all or were only partly clothed. After one year of the operation of the modification programmes, 91 per cent were almost always completely clothed. Comparable results were obtained in teaching them to feed themselves. Before the introduction of the programme only just over half the residents were capable of eating without assistance; after one year this proportion rose to 95 per cent. Useful improvements in cooperation between residents and in recreation, both solitary and cooperative, were also attained. Another striking outcome of the modification programme was the virtual elimination of aggressive, disruptive and injurious types of behaviour. Before the introduction of the programme, approximately half the residents would frequently assault others, but six months later this was rare.

Although few of the reports describing the successful introduction of these modification techniques have been carried out on such a large scale as that of the Faribault Hospital project, there is an encouraging uniformity of outcome. There really is no longer any doubt about the powerful effects this type of teaching programme can have in improving the skills of severely retarded people. In particular, these programmes can help them to gain much greater control over their own daily activities and functions, including the important ones of eating, maintaining continence and dressing themselves. Some useful advances have also been made in the teaching of low-grade but specific and useful occupational skills. A small measure of progress has been made in achieving improved social competence and more extensive recreational abilities. Needless to say, many questions remain.

What can be achieved by the widespread introduction of training schemes of this type? What is the best way to organise, implement and evaluate these schemes? Who should carry them out—and where? Allowing for variations in need according to region, country and facilities, we can attempt some answers.

We already are in possession of a technology capable of alleviating the squalor and degradation of severely retarded people, most of whom have to spend the greater part of their lives in residential institutions. It also seems likely that a vigorous implementation of extended versions of these programmes will make it possible for numbers of retarded people, who at the moment are in long-stay institutions, to return to live in the community. It is also clear that many more severely retarded people can be helped to acquire some useful if limited occupational skills. They can help to earn their keep and derive psychological and material benefits from that contribution. As the emphasis moves from custodial care to education and training, the provision of services for intellectually retarded people will be seen to fall more often into the province of education and less often into that of medicine. One can foresee a time in the not too distant future when, apart from the provision of ordinary medical cover available to other people in the population, many of the retarded people in our community will be assisted and supported by educational and social agencies exclusively.

Where in all this will psychologists fit in? One hopes that they will continue to contribute to the refinement and expansion of these and comparable modification techniques and that they will play an important part in the education of professionals whose exclusive job it will be to assist severely retarded people. We may even see the emergence of a new profession, the main function of which will be provision of support, education and other services for the intellectually retarded population, both within the community and for those who have to live in protected institutions. These new professionals will be comparable to teachers rather than to nurses as the emphasis continues to shift from medicine to education. As part of this changing trend, it is to be expected that the appointment of psychiatrists to undertake the supervision and care of intellectually retarded people will be discontinued. There are those who are understandably mystified by the fact that psychiatrists were ever called upon to undertake this type of function. Certainly, it is true that only a small minority of the intellectually retarded population have psychiatric problems as we generally understand them.

The severely retarded members of our population have always been accorded low priority in the social, health and education services. It would be unrealistic to expect this situation to change of a sudden, but we believe that a wider recognition of the improved psychological tools now available might promote the planning and implementation of more humane and effective services for these seriously underprivileged members of our community.

191

Although we have dealt almost exclusively with the application of the new technology to the training and education of severely retarded people in institutions, most of the ideas and techniques are equally applicable to assisting retarded people dwelling in the community. Considerable progress has been made in training parents and other relatives to use these techniques in their own homes. This new facility, coupled with the improved adjustments achieved by training within institutions, will ensure that more retarded people are enabled to live in the community. In this way we shall be able to avoid adding to the considerable handicaps of retarded people the debilitating effects of institutional life, which are now recognised to arise in almost all long-stay institutions. Assistance and education for severely retarded people who continue to live in the community need to be provided in three ways: parents and other relatives need encouragement to participate actively in attending training classes and demonstrations. Peripatetic nurse–teachers will have to carry out a good deal of their instruction and training in the homes of the people affected, and, thirdly, provision for concentrated periods of training needs to be made available at day-centres in order to cope with resistant forms of disruptive behaviour or handicaps which the person is slow to overcome.

12 Projects and prospects

Plans for expanding the contribution made by psychologists to the theory and practice of medicine are less likely to meet frank opposition than concealed scepticism. Coming from a well-established profession with its victories on display, an open-minded scepticism towards the ambitions of the newer science of psychology, should be accepted and even welcomed. It is largely up to psychologists to propose the plans and projects, to suggest ways in which their skills might be helpful.

Before discussing some of the practical obstacles to the infusion of psychology into medicine, we will describe a selection of worthwhile projects that could be undertaken without delay (indeed most of the topics have already been studied, to some extent). This 'shopping list' is, of course, indicative, not comprehensive. Most of the ideas have been referred to earlier in this book and are presented as both a reminder and a prompt.

Psychologists could carry out surveys of prevailing infant and child welfare clinics and other services, in the hope of identifying the most serious and common psychological and behaviour problems encountered by parents. In the light of this information, they could apply their extensive knowledge of child psychology and of behaviour modification to dealing with these problems. Having established and evaluated the necessary methodology, they could hand over a greatly improved style of service to the nursing, paediatric and other personnel involved. We are not referring here to psychiatric illnesses of childhood or even to what are regarded today as being psychiatric problems, but the day to day, month to month problems of child development—social, intellectual, psychomotor, self-care, continence training and the rest. If successful, this development would quickly grow into a genuinely preventive form of health care.

Ante-natal clinics are among the most common of the preventive medical services; they certainly provide the most intensive *preparation* for a medical experience. It is regrettable that this keen sense of the value of preparation has not been extended to other aspects of medical practice—perhaps repeated and convincing evaluations of ante-natal preparations may help to establish the general point in addition to the particular uses of ante-natal care. This assumes of course that the preparation is of value and while the available indications are favourable, we need confirmation. Further, the field is in need of careful weeding out and this can best be achieved by systematic evaluative studies. In our view, any evaluation which neglects the significant psychological processes involved in the various stages of childbirth—from early pregnancy to at least three months after the birth—will be of limited value and potentially misleading. Given the requisite cooperation from the pregnant woman, paediatricians and nurses, psychologists could make a helpful contribution here.

Admission to hospital is a distressing experience for many people and especially the young. As long as we retain the view that emotional reactions in hospital are a first-class nuisance, potentially or actually obstructing the investigatory or surgical procedures, they will continue to be just that—an obstructive nuisance. If, however, we remind ourselves that medical care is not simply the search for cures but fundamentally the alleviation of distress and pain—neither of which are solely 'physical' phenomena—then emotional reactions to hospitals and illnesses are very much the business of medical practice. As we have argued, there is good reason to believe (and even some slight evidence of a direct nature) that adequate preparation for hospital, and indeed any painful or unusual investigations and procedures, is capable of reducing distress and aiding recovery. We have also argued that this preparation is primarily a psychological matter. Specific proposals for improving preparations for hospital admissions and operations are given in Chapter 10.

The relationship between a patient and his doctor, so much emphasised in the medical literature and teaching texts, apparently exerts a major influence on the outcome of consultations and any ensuing treatment. There can be no debate about the fact that the nature of this relationship is essentially a psychological subject (unfortunately neglected outside psychiatry). This fascinating phenomenon is extremely complex and has proved to be difficult to study in a scientific manner, but it can and should be done—particularly, we feel, in the context of general practice. In the same province, the actual consultation sesssion is in need of detailed study. The value of these sessions is undoubtedly open to improvement. For example, we have referred to ways of improving the doctor's communications with his patient. The powerful influence of well-delivered and timely advice from a doctor makes study of the consultation process as worthwhile as it is interesting.

In Chapter 6 we discussed the factors which contribute to the uncanny power of placebos; the patient's attitude to his doctor is a central factor and psychologists could carry out a useful service by extending their study of placebo power, from psychiatry into the whole range of medical practices. In view of the overwhelming use of pills and tablets in current practice, the great majority of consultations ending with the prescription of drugs, the importance of an increased understanding of the psychology of pill-taking is self-evident.

The value of a satisfactory relationship between doctor and patient is suggested indirectly by the evidence on ways and means of giving up smoking and presumably, the relationship exerts a similar influence in related matters, such as avoiding certain foods, holding to diets, etc. Psychological research into smoking behaviour is well under way but little attention has been given to ways of achieving the necessary restraints on unhealthy eating patterns, dieting and the taking or avoiding of exercise (for example, in cases of cardiac disorder) and the many other behavioural prescriptions delivered by doctors. At first sight, none of them seem to pose any intellectual problems and improved methods of self-control can be expected before long.

Matching compassion with energy, psychologists might in future try to redirect more care and attention towards the chronically ill and disabled, particularly to older people. Some work, but still far too little, has been carried out in caring for the aged ill, and in rehabilitation of blind or deaf people, among others. For psychologists, however, rehabilitation need not be confined to the tradition of occupational rehabilitation. Psychological rehabilitation aims wider and includes mobility, social and sexual adjustment, friends and girl-friends, as well as a return to work. In many cases of handicap, chronic or sudden, the affected person needs to learn new ways of behaving, feeling and relating to people. Medical rehabilitation centres should have a psychological service—even if psychologists themselves

196

have first to show these establishments that they would benefit from a full service.

We need sensitive studies of the approach of death, including the taboos and profound fears attached to the subject. As a first step, it would be extremely valuable to have clarification of the question of doctors informing patients when they have a fatal illness. At present there seems to be a gulf between doctors and their patients, the former aiming to protect through ignorance and the patients resenting the concealment. Psychologists could play a major part in clearing up some of these problems, by working towards the identification of when to tell, whom to tell and how to tell. There are few more distressing problems in the field of medicine than these and they unquestionably need sympathetic and tactful study.

Doctors are, of course, also faced with the need to inform people of other types of misfortune, such as the diagnosis of crippling, chronic and incurable illnesses. Investigation of these topics will presumably reveal the same gap between the wishes of the majority to be told the full facts and their doctors' reluctance to do so. Psychologists could assist in analysing why this reluctance occurs, and its consequences. Common explanations offered by doctors are that the information would cause unnecessary distress, or be misunderstood, or be resented —or all three. No doubt any and all of these reactions do occur, but it does not follow that silence or concealment are the only courses open. Working in collaboration with psychologists, doctors could develop methods of conveying news of misfortunes in a way that minimises misunderstandings and comforts the distressed. We all need to learn a great deal more about how to help people to accept misfortune and how to cope with it; perhaps the progress made in reducing anxiety and depression will provide a helpful starting point. The beliefs that problems of death and misfortune cannot be studied in a detached manner and, further, that each doctor intuitively acts in the best way open to him, are not satisfactory. In dealing with these problems, doctors sometimes belittle themselves, not least by their inclination to deny that a significant reason for their reluctance to give painful news is that it is often a distressing and distasteful experience for them. Medical students and doctors could benefit from systematic preparation and counselling for this difficult part of their duties.

Professional cooperation: in a desire to contribute their knowledge and skills to medicine, psychologists may be inclined to exaggerate both—while losing sight of their ignorance of medical subjects. Somehow they need to achieve a balance between enthusiasm and humility. While some doctors welcome cooperation from psychologists, others regard the notion with suspicion; the majority are likely to await events with one or other variety of scepticism. Some doctors fear that psychologists will intrude into the special relationship they have with their patients. Others are worried that, when psychologists work directly with patients, their own clinical responsibility may be eroded. These complex questions cannot be explored at length here and although reassurance on the first fear is easily given, the fact is that psychologists and other para-medicals have already accepted a measure of clinical responsibility. Any person who gives a professional service to a patient assumes at least some clinical responsibility for his actions. Clinical responsibility is not a unitary concept, not a single indivisible lump. Each member of a medical team is responsible for his professional actions and it is hard to see how it could be otherwise. It does not follow that doctors are losing in this process or that the interests of their patients are jeopardised. As the primary agent in the medical team, the doctor usually is in over-all responsibility and in any event, he needs to ensure that his patient is assisted by suitably qualified and registered professionals.

We have devoted most of this chapter to proposals for psychological research but the need for inter-professional cooperation is even greater in service work—provided in hospitals, clinics and consulting rooms. Despite some persisting difficulties, psychologists and psychiatrists have established a useful clinical partnership and one can easily foresee how mutually valuable working relationships could also grow between paediatricians and psychologists, neurologists and psychologists and so on. Specialised clinics are among the most likely places for the growth of these contributory partnerships and we can use pain clinics as an illustration. The neurologist and physician between them would arrive at a diagnosis and prescribe the necessary pills and/or surgery or whatever else is felt to be required. The persistence of the patient's pain in the face of these measures might signal the need for a more individual approach, taking into account his personality and present circumstances, his understanding of his illness and the accompanying emotion, and so on. These are psychological matters and their proper analysis might afford the patient some reassurance and comfort; in some cases, specific psychological methods might help to reduce the intensity and/or frequency of the pain, or modify the pain behaviour, or increase or decrease pain complaints as necessary. Bearing in mind the more comprehensive theory of pain discussed in Chapter 3, there is good reason to hope that treatment directed at the upper, cognitive centres of the nervous system can benefit patients. Even in advance of a systematic attack on the

199

problem, psychologists can offer several practical ideas for pain control. Anxiety-reduction methods will probably help some patients, especially those with neurotic and extraverted personalities (who are known to complain more about their pains). The biofeedback method described in Chapter 7 is being turned towards the treatment of headaches and muscular pains, powerful suggestions (especially from a highly regarded doctor) can reduce pain; increased understanding and predictability of pain events can reduce subjective pain. There will be no shortage of ideas.

It would be a disservice to pretend that conflicts do not and will not occur, especially during the period of transition. The process of absorbing a new and vigorous science into the health service will be uncomfortable, even while it helps to improve patient care and invigorate the theory of medicine. As members of the more powerful and better established of the two disciplines, medical personnel can afford to be more accommodating and flexible—not an easy task for people educated in a firmly hierarchical profession. For their part, psychologists might avoid the pattern of grumbling grievances which surfaced from time to time in their psychiatric period. At the administrative planning level, the infusion of psychology into medicine will probably be achieved sooner and with fewer collisions if the provision of psychological services is organised and ordered at a very high level rather than within a single hospital or within small medical units. This is particularly desirable during the expected period of rapid change. Strategic planning can only be carried out at an executive level. The transfer of psychologists between projects, services and specialities will require executive action, rather than a barter system within local hospitals.

Finally, it is well to remember that despite the conservative structure of their profession, doctors have shown themselves to be particularly responsive to useful clinical innovations.

Summing up: the potential benefits

Having urged a fundamental change in the scope of medical psychology, we must outline the benefits which might follow if our proposals were to be implemented.

Doctors can expect to benefit in three respects. The infusion of psychological influences into medical practice would certainly restore part of the human interest which has been drained away by the advances of technological medicine. These advances, combined with growing demands for medical help, reduce the time available for individual patients and also serve to limit each doctor's range of therapeutic service-skills. Recognition of the important role of psychological factors in doctor–patient relationships, and their inevitable practical consequences, would help to restore the waning personal contacts of practising doctors. It will, of course, entail spending more time with each patient as a prerequisite for relating to him as a person—bearing in mind that the patient, not the doctor, has the greatest responsibility for his own health. It will be objected, of course, that it is the doctor's *time* which is in shortest supply at present and that to ask for more of it is absurdly unrealistic. So it is; if the prevailing forms of practice continue unaltered, there is little hope of nurturing the desired psychological relations between patient and doctor. In our view, medical practice *can* change in the desired direction and time can be found for more personal consultations and exchanges. Our two

201

suggestions are neither novel nor exclusive and, worse luck, they cannot be introduced quickly.

In the first place, a concerted programme of health education should be undertaken in order to train all of us to accept greater responsibility for our own bodies; doctors need only be consulted when signs of serious difficulty appear. We know that the majority of visits made to family doctors are for minor pains, coughs, colds and the like. These visits can be greatly reduced by education, given intensively at school and through the media, which would explain basic human physiology and the signs and symptoms of the statistically most common complaints. People could be told, clearly and often, when to seek professional help and what to do before it arrives or instead of it. In addition to public education, doctors need to do even more to educate their own patients and return some responsibility to them. Both private and public education would inevitably help to diminish those persisting aspects of medical paternalism, while helping to reverse the steadily increasing demands for medical help.

Secondly, the trends towards developing more and better ancillary workers can be accelerated. They can relieve doctors of part of their extensive clinical commitments in order to restore more *intensive* and prolonged therapeutic relationships. This book has indicated numerous ways, direct and indirect, in which clinical psychologists can help doctors to cope with clinical demands. The most obvious and easily implemented of the direct psychological services include those pertaining to developmental and behavioural problems of childhood, sexual problems, sleep disorders, mild anxiety. Indirect help can be given by improving the treatment and control of pain (including headaches), compliance with medical advice, placing drug prescribing and imbibing on a more rational basis, and so on.

Psychology can also benefit medicine as a whole by contributing to theories of illness, concepts of sickness behaviour, patient-doctor relations, the theory of pain and its alleviation, the nature of insanity and how it differs from disorders of behaviour, the behaviour and feelings of doctors, patients' expectations and satisfactions, preparation for pain and for death, and many other critical subjects. Psychologists, by virtue of the emphasis placed on research in the psychology syllabus, have a particularly useful contribution to make and need merely to receive an invitation.

Patients could benefit from the greater use of psychology and psychologists in a general way—through the elevation of standards of care—and in a special way from a widening of our conception of what patients should receive from their doctors. In addition to skilled technical aid, patients needs comfort and sympathy, preferably of a non-paternalistic brand. People want more information about their ailments, the tests they undergo, the drugs they take, their prognosis. All of these needs are far more likely to be met by doctors who are trained to recognise their patients' psychological needs as well as their bodily dysfunctions. Patients would experience less pain and less distress if they were given adequate preparation for operations, investigations and hospital admissions—and 'adequate preparation' is primarily a psychological matter.

Acceptance of our wider view of the role of clinical psychologists would benefit that profession immeasurably. Indeed, it is our opinion that unless psychologists accept these new challenges, their profession is unlikely to attain maturity. There is little to be said, either professionally or intellectually, for a highly trained group of people choosing to remain in the shadow of a single specialised branch of medicine. If they aspire to be junior psychiatrists, or junior doctors of any sort, psychologists are bound to be worn by perpetual frustration, while at the same time arousing the worst suspicions in their medical colleagues. Psychologists are sometimes accused of wishing to act like doctors, and worse, of wanting to further this ambition deviously. It can be admitted that some (many?) clinical psychologists are frustrated doctors, but the new form of psychology proposed here could more than satisfy their not ignoble ambitions. In so far as they share with members of the medical profession a desire to relieve distress and provide comfort for people in difficulty, there will be ample opportunity for them to work towards their aims. What distinguishes their speciality is the central importance of psychological factors. If clinical psychologists insist on working their own ground —the subjective, personal and behavioural aspects of health and sickness—the next decade could be by far the most rewarding and exciting in the short history of their emerging profession.

Notes

1 PSYCHOLOGY IN MEDICINE

1 Office of Health Economics, no. 43, *Medicine and Society*, 1972
2 M. Shepherd, S. Mitchell and B. Oppenheim, *Childhood Behaviour and Mental Health*, London University Press, 1971
3 H. J. Eysenck and S. Rachman, *Bulletin of the British Psychological Society*, vol. 26, 1973, 1130
4 R. Hetherington, *Bulletin of the British Psychological Society*, vol. 20, 1967, 1
5 P. Ley, *Bulletin of the British Psychological Society*, vol. 25, 1972, 115
6 P. Ley, *Proceedings of the British Association for the Advancement of Science*, September 1971
7 G. Patterson and M. Gullion, *Living with Children*, Research Press, Illinois, 1972
8 G. Patterson, *Families*, Research Press, Illinois, 1971
9 L. Hoffman and M. Hoffman, *Review of Child Development Research*, vols 1 and 2, Russell Sage Fund, New York, 1964 and 1966

2 DOCTOR'S ORDERS

1 B. Korsch and V. Negrete, *Scientific American*, 227, 1972, 66
2 P. Ley, *Bulletin of the British Psychological Society*, vol. 25, 1972
3 P. Ley, *Proceedings of the British Association for the Advancement of Science*, 1974
4 C. Fletcher, *Communication in Medicine*, Nuffield Hospital Trust, 1973

205

Notes

5 J. Aitken-Swan and E. Easson, *British Medical Journal*, 1, 1959, 779
6 P. Ley and S. Spelman, *Communicating with the Patient*, Staples Press, 1967
7 R. K. Turner, G. Young and S. Rachman, *Behaviour Research and Therapy*, 8, 1970, 367
8 P. Ley, *Psychological Medicine*, 3, 1973, 217
9 H. Williams, *Practitioner*, 202, 1969
10 H. Leventhal, *Advances in Experimental Social Psychology*, ed. L. Berkowitz, Academic Press, New York, 1970
11 I. Janis and S. Feshbach, *Journal of Abnormal and Social Psychology*, 48, 1953, 78
12 H. Leventhal *et al.*, *Journal of Personality and Social Psychology*, 6, 1967, 313
13 S. Rachman, *Bibliotheca Nutritio et Dieta*, no. 14, *Malnutrition is a Problem of Ecology*, ed. G. György, 1970

3 PAIN

1 R. Melzack, *The Puzzle of Pain*, Penguin Books, 1973
2 H. K. Beecher, *Measurement of Subjective Responses*, Oxford University Press, 1959
3 W. K. Livingstone, *Pain Mechanisms*, Macmillan, 1943
4 R. Melzack, A. Z. Wetsz and L. T. Sprague, *Experimental Neurology*, 8, 1963, 239–47
5 S. B. Cheng and L. K. Ding, *Nature*, 27 April 1973, 242
6 H. Merskey, unpublished thesis, Oxford University, 1964
7 M. R. Bond and I. Pilowsky, *Journal of Psychosomatic Research*, 10, 1966, 203
8 J. D. Hardy, H. G. Wolff and H. Goodell, *Pain Sensations and Reactions*, Williams & Wilkins, New York, 1952
9 K. Woodrow *et al.*, *Psychosomatic Medicine*, 34, 1972, 548
10 I. Janis, *Stress and Frustration*, Harcourt Brace, New York, 1971, ch. 9
11 M. R. Bond, *British Journal of Psychiatry*, 119, 1971, 553
12 R. Lynn and H. J. Eysenck, *Perceptual and Motor Skills*, 12, 1961, 161–2
13 S. B. G. Eysenck, *Journal of Mental Science*, 107, 1961, 417–30

Notes

14 A. Petrie, *Individuality in Pain and Suffering*, University of Chicago Press, 1967

15 H. J. Eysenck, *The Biological Basis of Personality*, Thomas, Springfield, 1971

16 W. E. Fordyce, R. S. Fowler and B. Delateur, *Behaviour Research and Therapy*, 6, 1968, 105–7

4 A PSYCHOLOGICAL APPROACH TO HEADACHES

1 W. E. Waters, *Headache*, 4, 1970, 178–86

2 A. M. Ostfeld, *The Common Headache Syndromes: Biochemistry, Pathophysiology, Therapy*, C. C. Thomas, Illinois, 1962

3 Office of Health Economics, no. 41, 1972

4 H. G. Wolff, *Headache and other Head Pain*, Oxford University Press, 1963

5 A. P. Friedman, *Journal of American Medical Association*, 179, 1962, 717–18

6 A. P. Friedman, *Neurology*, 4, 1964, 773–88

7 A. P. Friedman, *Journal of American Medical Association*, 190, 1964, 445–7

8 W. E. Waters, *British Medical Journal*, 2, 1971, 77–81

9 P. Sainsbury and J. G. Gibson, *Journal of Neurology, Neurosurgery and Psychiatry*, 17, 1954, 216

10 H. Selensky, *Bulletin of New York Academy of Medicine*, 15, 1939, 757

11 M. J. Martin *et al.*, in *Studies in Headache—Research and Clinical*, ed. A. P. Friedman, Karger, Basle, vol. 1, 1967

12 A. M. Ostfeld, *American Journal of Medical Sciences*, 241, 1961, 192

13 A. P. Friedman, *Neurology*, 13, 1963, 27–33

14 O. Appenzeller, K. Davidson and J. Marshall, *Journal of Neurology, Neurosurgery and Psychiatry*, 26, 1962, 447

15 I. D. Balshan, *Archives of General Psychiatry*, 7, 1962, 436–48

16 R. Melzack and W. S. Torgenson, *Anaesthesiology*, 34, 1971, 50

17 S. Rachman, *The Meanings of Fear*, Penguin Books, 1974

18 W. E. Fordyce, R. S. Fowler and B. Delateur, *Behaviour, Research and Therapy*, 6, 1968, 105–7

Notes

5 SLEEP DISORDERS

1 K. Dunnell and A. Cartwright, *Medicine Takers, Prescribers and Hoarders*, Routledge & Kegan Paul, 1972
2 M. Shepherd *et al.*, *Psychiatric Illness in General Practice*, Oxford University Press, 1966
3 D. Dunlop, *British Medical Bulletin*, 26, 1970, 236
4 H. G. Jones and I. Oswald, *Electroencephalography and Clinical Neurophysiology*, 24, 1968, 378
5 I. Oswald, *Sleep*, Penguin Books, 1966
6 N. Kleitman, *Sleep and Wakefulness*, University of Chicago Press, 1963
7 H. L. Williams *et al.*, *Psychophysiology*, 3, 1966, 164–75
8 R. T. Wilkinson in *Progress in Clinical Psychology*, ed. L. A. Abt and B. F. Reiss, Grune & Stratton, New York, 1969
9 A. Kales, *Sleep: Physiology and Pathology*, Lippincott, New York, 1969
10 D. R. Hawkins, *Sleep and Dreaming*, ed. E. Hartmann, Little, Brown, Boston, 1970
11 P. Hauri, in Hartmann, ed., *op. cit.*
12 B. A. Schwartz, G. Guilband and H. Fischgeld, *Presse Med.*, 71, 1963, 1474
13 L. J. Monroe, *Journal of Abnormal Psychology*, 74, 1967, 255
14 T. D. Borkovec and D. C. Fowles, *Journal of Abnormal Psycology*, 1, 1973, 153–8
15 S. W. Steinmark and T. D. Borkovec, *Progressive Relaxation Training*, ed. T. D. Borkovec and D. A. Bernstein, Research Press, Illinois, 1973
16 R. Turner, G. Young and S. Rachman, *Behaviour Research and Therapy*, 8, 1970, 376
17 B. Hallgren, *Acta Psychiatrica et Neurologica (Scandinavica)*, 31, 1956, 379
18 R. Lapouse and M. Monk, *American Journal of Orthopsychiatry*, 29, 1959, 803
19 A. MacFarlane *et al.*, *A Developmental Study of Behaviour Problems in Normal Children*, University of California Press, 1954
20 S. Lovibond, *Conditioning and Enuresis*, Pergamon Press, 1964

Notes

21   G. Young and R. K. Turner, *Health and Social Service Journal*, April 1973, 793
22   G. DeLeon and W. Mandell, *Journal of Clinical Psychology*, 22, 1966, 326
23   J. Werry and J. Cohrssen, *Journal of Pediatrics*, 67, 1965, 423
24   H. G. Jones in *Behaviour Therapy and the Neuroses*, ed. H. J. Eysenck, Pergamon Press, 1960
25   H. J. Eysenck and S. Rachman, *Causes and Cures of Neurosis*, Routledge & Kegan Paul, 1965
26   R. K. Turner *et al.*, *Behaviour, Research and Therapy*, 8, 1970, 376
27   W. Finley *et al.*, *Behaviour, Research and Therapy*, 11, 1973, 289
28   C. Fisher, *et al.*, *Journal of American Psychoanalytic Association*, 18, 1970, 4

6   PLACEBO POWER

1   K. Dunnell and A. Cartwright, *Medicine Takers, Prescribers and Hoarders*, Routledge & Kegan Paul, 1972
2   D. Dunlop, *British Medical Bulletin*, 26, 1970, 236–9
3   O. Wade, *British Medical Bulletin*, 26, 1970, 240
4   D. Rosenhan, *Science*, 179, 1973, 250
5   R. Bell, *Woman in Health and Sickness*, 5th edn, Newnes, 1923
6   A. Miller, M. Phil. Dissertation, University of London, 1973
7   N. Brill, *Archives of General Psychiatry*, 10, 1964, 581
8   L. Park and L. Covi, *Archives of General Psychiatry*, 12, 1965, 336
9   A. Shapiro, *Handbook of Psychotherapy and Behaviour Change*, eds. A. Bergin and S. Garfield, Wiley, New York, 1971, ch. 12
10   J. Frank, *Persuasion and Healing*, rev. edn, Johns Hopkins University Press, 1973
11   G. Paul, *Insight versus Desensitization*, Stanford University Press, 1966
12   G. Young and R. Turner, *Behaviour Research and Therapy*, 3, 1965, 93

13 C. Joyce, *Proceedings of the Royal Society of Medicine,* vol. 55, 1962, 776

14 G. Foulds, *Journal of Mental Science,* 104, 1958, 259

15 G. Uhlenhuth *et al., American Journal of Psychiatry,* 115, 1959, 905

7 SELF-CONTROL OF BODILY FUNCTIONS

1 N. E. Miller, *Science,* 163, 1969, 434–45

2 M. Wenger and B. Bajchi, *Behavioural Science,* 6, 1961, 312–23

3 A. Koestler, *The Lotus and the Robot,* Hutchinson, 1960

4 N. E. Miller in *Biofeedback and Self-Control,* ed. T. X. Barber *et al.,* Aldine Publishing Co., Chicago, 1970

5 D. Shapiro, B. Tursky and G. E. Schwartz, *Circulation Research,* supplement I, 26, 27, 1970, 1–27 to 1–32

6 B. T. Engel, *Psychophysiology,* 9, 1972, 161–77

7 M. W. Headrick, B. W. Feather and D. T. Wells, *Psychophysiology,* 8, 1971, 132–42

8 D. Shapiro, B. Tursky and G. E. Schwartz, *Psychosomatic Medicine,* 32, 1970, 417–23

9 D. Shapiro, H. Benson, B. Tursky and G. E. Schwartz, *Science,* 173, 1971, 740–42

10 D. Shapiro *et al.,* 1971, *Psychophysiology,* 9, 1972, 296–304

11 H. D. Kimmel, *Psychological Bulletin,* 67, 1967, 337–45

12 J. V. Basmajian, *Science,* 141, 1963, 440–41

13 T. H. Budzynski and J. M. Stoyva, *Journal of Applied Behaviour Analysis,* 2, 1969, 231–7

14 J. J. Lynch and D. A. Paskewitz, *Journal of Nervous and Mental Disease,* 153, 1971, 205–17

15 P. B. Fenwick, *Electroencephalography and Clinical Neurophysiology,* 21, 1966, 618

16 A. Maslow, *American Psychologist,* 24, 1969, 724–35

17 T. Weiss and B. T. Engel, *Psychosomatic Medicine,* 33, no. 4, 1971, 301–23

18 T. H. Budzynski, *Journal of Behaviour Therapy and Experimental Psychiatry,* 1, 1970, 202–11

19 A. Jacob and R. Felton, *Archives of Physical Medicine,* 50, 1969, 34–9

Notes

8 REDUCING HEALTH RISKS BY SELF-CONTROL

1 M. Russell, *Nursing Times*, May 1972
2 E. Abramson, *Behaviour Research and Therapy*, vol. 12, 1974
3 A. McKennell and R. Thomas, *Adults and Adolescents' Smoking Habits and Attitudes*, HMSO, 1967
4 J. Bynner, *The Young Smoker*, HMSO, 1969
5 M. Russell, *British Medical Journal*, vol. 2, 1971
6 M. Russell, *British Journal of Medical Psychology*, vol. 44, 1971
7 W. Dunn, *Smoking Behavior*, Winston, Washington, DC, 1973
8 H. J. Eysenck, *Personality and the Maintenance of the Smoking Habit* in Dunn, ed., *op. cit.*
9 D. Bernstein, *Psychological Bulletin*, vol. 71, 1969
10 S. Rachman, 'The modification of attitudes and behaviour', *Bibliotheca Nutritio et Dieta*, 14, 1970
11 M. Russell, *British Medical Journal*, vol. 1, 1970
12 H. Williams, *Practitioner*, 202, 1969
13 M. Raw, Unpublished dissertation, University of London, 1974
14 A. Stunkard, *New York Journal of Medicine*, vol. 58, 1958
15 S. Schachter, *American Psychologist*, vol. 26, 1971
16 S. Schachter, *Emotion, Obesity and Crime*, Academic Press, New York, 1971
17 A. Stunkard, *Archives of General Psychiatry*, vol. 26, 1972
18 G. Ferster *et al.*, *Journal Mathetics*, vol. 1, 1962
19 R. Stuart, *Behaviour Research and Therapy*, vol. 5, 1967
20 R. Stuart, *Behaviour Research and Therapy*, vol. 9, 1971
21 S. Penick *et al.*, *Psychosomatic Medicine*, vol. 33, 1971

9 PSYCHIATRIC PSYCHOLOGY

1 J. Zubin, L. Efron and F. Schumer, *An Experimental Approach to Projective Tests*, Wiley, New York, 1965
2 H. J. Eysenck in *Recent Advances in Psychiatry*, ed. G. Fleming, Churchill, 1958
3 K. Little and E. Shneidman, *Psychological Monographs*, vol. 73, no. 476, 1959

211

4 S. Rachman, *The Effects of Psychotherapy,* Pergamon Press, 1971
5 C. Rogers, *Journal of Consulting Psychology,* 21, 1957, 95
6 S. Rachman, *Psychological Bulletin,* 67, 1967, 93
7 H. J. Eysenck, *Behaviour Therapy and the Neuroses,* Pergamon Press, 1969
8 S. Rachman, 'Psychological Treatment' in *Handbook of Abnormal Psychology,* ed. H. J. Eysenck, 2nd edn., Pitman, 1972
9 S. Rachman and J. Teasdale, *Aversion Therapy and Behaviour Disorders,* Routledge & Kegan Paul, 1969
10 I. Marks, *Fears and Phobias,* Heinemann, 1969
11 V. Meyer and E. Chesser, *Behaviour Therapy in Clinical Psychiatry,* Penguin Books, 1970
12 C. Franks, ed. *Behaviour Therapy,* McGraw-Hill, New York, 1971
13 R. Kendell, *British Journal of Hospital Medicine,* 6, 1971, 147
14 S. Rachman, *New Society,* April 1973
15 A. Bergin in *Handbook of Psychotherapy and Behavior Change,* eds. A. Bergin and S. Garfield, Wiley, New York, 1970
16 J. Frank in *The Role of Learning in Psychotherapy,* ed. R. Porter, Churchill, 1968
17 A. Bandura, *The Principles of Behaviour Modification,* Holt, Rinehart & Winston, New York, 1969
18 Memorandum of a Working Party set up by the Royal College of Psychiatrists, *British Journal of Psychiatry,* September 1973
19 D. Rosenhan, *Science,* 179, 1973, 250

10 THE PSYCHOLOGICAL IMPACT OF ADMISSION TO HOSPITAL

1 I. Janis, *Stress and Frustration,* Harcourt Brace, New York, 1971
2 R. Lazarus, *Psychological Stress and the Coping Process,* McGraw-Hill, New York, 1966
3 S. Rachman, *The Meanings of Fear,* Penguin Books, 1974

Notes

4 L. Egbert *et al., New England Journal of Medicine,* 270, 1964, 825

5 R. Davie, N. Butler and H. Goldstein, *From Birth to Seven,* Longmans, 1972.

6 *Lancet,* Editorial, 2, 1967, 1929

7 B. Wood, Y. Wong and C. Theodoridis, *Lancet,* 2, 1972, 645

8 M. Rutter, *Maternal Deprivation Reassessed,* Penguin Books, 1972

9 L. Yarrow in *Review of Child Development Research,* ed. L. and E. Hoffman, Russell Sage, New York, 1964

10 M. Stacey *et al., Hospitals, Children and their Families,* Routledge & Kegan Paul, 1970

11 S. Rachman, *Behaviour Therapy,* 3, 1972, 379

12 D. Prugh *et al., American Journal of Orthopsychiatry,* 23, 1953, 70

13 P. Moran, Thesis, Yale University, 1963. Quoted by Janis, *op. cit*

11 CUSTODIANS OR TEACHERS

1 T. Thompson and J. Grabowski, eds., *Behaviour Modification of the Mentally Retarded,* Oxford University Press, 1972, p. 7

2 S. Rachman, *Journal of Child Psychology and Child Psychiatry,* 3, 1962, 149

3 H. J. Eysenck and S. Rachman, *The Causes and Cures of Neurosis,* Routledge & Kegan Paul, 1965

4 B. F. Skinner, *Science and Human Behavior,* Macmillan, New York, 1953

5 B. F. Skinner, *Beyond Freedom and Dignity,* Penguin Books, 1973

6 T. Ayllon and N. Azrin, *The Token Economy,* Appleton-Century-Crofts, New York, 1968

7 T. Ayllon and J. Michael, *Journal of Experimental Analysis of Behaviour,* 2, 1959, 323

8 M. Wolf, T. Risley and H. Mees, *Behaviour Research and Therapy,* 1, 1964, 305

9 R. Foxx and N. Azrin, *Toilet Training the Retarded,* Research Press, Illinois, 1973

10 G. Bigelow in Thompson and Grabowski, *op. cit.*

Acknowledgements

We wish to thank Professor Neal Miller and Dr T. Thompson for kindly granting permission to quote from their work, and their publishers (The American Association for the Advancement of Science and Oxford University Press respectively) for their agreement.

Index

Abnormal behaviour, 37, 138, 148, 149, 151, 154, 160, 164
Abramson, 211
Aching, 60, 67
Acupuncture, 45, 104
Adenoids, 170
Aitken-Swan, 24, 206
Alcoholism, 147
Alpha rhythms, 72, 82, 114, 119
American Psychiatric Association, 147
Analgesia, 45
Analgesics, 46, 51
Ante-natal clinics, 194
Anti-tetanus, 34
Anxiety, 43, 46, 51, 53, 55, 96, 144
Anxiety-reduction (see fear-reduction)
Appenzeller, 207
Attitude change, 35, 128
Attrition rate, 137
Audio-analgesia, 44
Augmenters, 49
Autism, 154
Autonomic nervous system, 104, 107–8, 111
Aversion, 129, 135, 144, 147
Ayllon, 180–1, 213
Azrin, 183, 184, 186, 187, 213

Bajchi, 106, 210
Balshan, 66, 207
Bandura, 212

Barbiturates, 82, 90
Basmajian, 114, 210
Bed-wetting (enuresis), 27, 70, 84–5
  and maladjustment, 84
  bell-and-pad treatment of, 85
  prevalence of, 84
  psychotherapy for, 85
Beecher, 38, 41, 46, 49–50, 51, 206
Behavioural genetics, 18
Behavioural prescriptions, 196
Behaviour modification therapy, 142, 147, 164, 193
Bell, 94–5, 107, 209
Benson, 210
Bergin, 157, 212
Bernstein, 128, 211
Bigelow, 188, 213
Biofeedback, 55, 67, 104, 116, 118, 119, 121–2, 200
Birmingham Children's Hospital, 170
Blood pressure, 62, 113–14, 115, 116–17
Bond, 47, 48, 206
Borkovec, 81, 208
Bowels, 94, 95, 107
Bowlby, 170
Brain-waves, 72–3
Brengelmann, 128
Brill, 96, 209
Bronchitics, 22
Budzynski, 114, 210
Butler, 169, 213
Bynner, 211

California University, 96, 167
Cardiac arrhythmia, 116
Care and cure, 163, 164
Carotids, 60
Cartwright, 92, 208, 209
Causalgia, 40, 41
Central nervous system, 108
Cervix, 48
Cheng, 45, 206
Chesser, 147, 212
Chest clinic, 130
Chest complaints, 33
Chest X-ray, 34
Child development, 17, 18, 194
Child guidance, 15, 85
Child psychology, 17–18, 193
Child welfare services, 17, 193, 202
Chinese traditional medicine, 45
Chiropractors, 158
Clinical responsibility, 150, 198
Cohrssen, 209
Cold pressor test, 44
Communication, 22, 24, 25, 29, 30, 195
Communication with doctors, 30, 32–3, 195
Community sample, 56
Conceptual tests, 142
Constipation, 94, 95
Consultations, 23, 26, 27, 31
Counselling, 158
Covi, 96, 209
Custodial care, 178, 190

Davidson, 207
Davie, 169, 213
Death, 197, 198, 203
Delateur, 207
DeLeon, 209
Dental care, 19, 34
Dentists, 19, 45
Depression, 29, 155, 156
Dervishes, 38, 44

Desensitisation, 52, 68, 144
De-synchrony, 68
Diabetics, 22, 27
Diagnosis, 26, 28, 140–1, 143, 161
Diet, 24, 32, 100
Ding, 45, 206
Distraction, 52, 55
Doctor-patient relationship, 22–33, 195–7, 201–2
Doctors' discontent, 22, 30, 33
Double blind control, 98
Dream cycles, 75
Dreams, 85–7
Dunlop, 71, 90, 91, 93, 208, 209
Dunn, 211
Dunnell, 92, 208, 209
Dying, 24, 197

Easson, 24, 206
Eating, 18
EEG, 86, 105, 115
Efron, 211
Egbert, 167, 213
Electrical resistance of skin, 114
Elimination, 18
Empathy, 26
Engel, 116, 210
Enuresis (*see* bed-wetting)
Epilepsy, 118
Ergotamine, 64
Exercises, 24, 100, 133
Extraverts, 49, 127
Eysench, H. J., 49, 127, 143, 205, 206, 209, 211, 212, 213
Eysenck, S. B. G., 49, 206

Family doctor (*see* general practitioner)
Faribault State Hospital, 178, 179, 188, 189
Fatigue, 80
Fear, 19, 144–8, 166, 177, 197

Fear-reduction, 19, 144–8, 200, 202
Feather, 210
Feedback techniques, 82
Felton, 118, 210
Fenwick, 210
Ferster, 136, 211
Feshbach, 206
Finley, 209
Fischgeld, 208
Fisher, 85, 209
Fletcher, 23, 205
Flooding, 68, 83, 144–5
Fordyce, 54, 207
Foulds, 100, 210
Fowler, 207
Fowles, 81, 208
Foxx, 183–7, 213
Frank, 157, 209, 212
Franks, 147, 212
Freud, 151
Friedman, 58, 62, 64, 207
Frontalis muscle, 65, 66

Galen, 98
General practice, 30, 56, 96, 102
General practitioner, 25, 32, 33, 57, 80, 130
Gibson, 207
Goldstein, 169, 213
Goodell, 206
Grabowski, 213
Gray, Henry, 158
Gray, Jeffrey, 158
Grievances, 200
Group techniques, 19
Guilbaud, 208
Gullion, 205

Hal, the case of, 184–6
Hallgren, 208
Handwashing, compulsive, 159
Hardy, 47, 206
Hartlepool, 90

Hauri, 76, 208
Hawkins, 76, 208
Headaches, 56–69, 115, 117–18
and personality, 58, 62, 63
pills for, 56–7
research on, 64–9
Special committee on, 58–9
sufferers of, 59, 62
tension, 64, 66, 121
types of, 58–9, 61, 65
unilateral, 59
vascular, 65
Head-banging, 70
Headrick, 210
Healers, religious, 158
Health education, 184–7
Heart pain, 42
Heart rate control, 115–16
Hetherington, 205
Hoffman, 205
Homosexuality, 150
Hospital, 18, 21–9
admissions, 161, 165–77, 195
children in, 169–77
Hygienic habits, 19, 94–5
Hypnotics (drugs), 70–1, 75, 76, 80
Hysteria, 94

Illness, 13, 14, 28, 52
frequency, 14, 15
Incontinence, 183–89
Indigestion, 42
Infant welfare, 193
Injurious behaviour, 39, 53, 189 (*see also* self-mutilation)
Ink-blots, 37, 139
Insanity, 160–3
Insomnia, 70, 71, 75, 76, 77–82, 88
Instrumental learning, 107–12
Insulin, 27
Intelligence, 29, 62, 139, 142
Intensity of stimulation, 41

Intestines, 107, 110
Introverts, 49, 127

Jacob, 118, 210
Janis, 48, 165, 166, 206, 212
Jargon, 26
Jones, 208, 209
Joyce, 100, 210

Kales, 75, 208
Kendell, 161, 212
Kimmel, 210
Kinaesthetic tests, 49
Kleitman, 73, 208
Koestler, 107, 210
Korsakoff's syndrome, 153
Korsch, 25, 26, 29, 205

Lancet, 170, 213
Lapouse, 208
Laxatives, 93–5
Lay knowledge, 28
Lazarus, 167, 212
Leucotomy, 46
Leventhal, 34, 206
Ley, 23, 24, 27–9, 205, 206
Little, 140, 211
Livingstone, 40, 206
Lobeline, 128
Los Angeles, 25
Lovibond, 208
Lumbar puncture, 26
Lung cancer, 34
Lynch, 210
Lynn, 49, 206

MacFarlane, 208
Marks, 147, 212
Marshall, 207
Martin, 62, 207
Masculine behaviour, 47
Maslow, 115, 210
Max Planck Institute, 128
McGill University, 119
McKennell, 211

Medical models, 142, 151–63
Medical psychology, 15, 16, 201
Medical schools, 15
Medicine and society, 14
Mees, 181, 213
Melzack, 37, 41, 53, 67, 206, 207
Mendell, 209
Mental conflicts, 58
Mental illness, 151–63
Mental rehearsal, 167
Mental X-rays, 139
Merskey, 206
Meyer, 147, 212
Michael, 213
Migraine, 57, 59, 64
   classical, 59, 63
Miller, 104, 107, 210
Minimum effort, 132
Mitchell, 205
MMPI, 139
Modelling, 144–6, 175–6
Monk, 208
Monroe, 208
Moran, 213
Morphine, 38, 46, 168
Mothers, 25, 26, 28
Muscle action potential, 114–6, 118
Muscle tension, 61
Muscular contraction head-aches, 58, 59, 60
Muscular relaxants, 64

Nausea, 57, 60
Neck, 65
Negrete, 25, 26, 29, 205
Neuralgias, 40, 41
Neurologists, 57, 58, 199
Neurosis, 143–4, 152
Neurotic patients, 46, 143–4
Nightmares, 70, 75, 83, 85–7
Night terrors, 70
Non-directive psychotherapy, 143

Obesity, 133–7
Obsessions, 145–6, 159
Office of Health Economics (OHE), 14, 15, 205, 207
Operant conditioning, 18, 144–8, 180–90
Operations, 51, 167–70
Oppenheim, 205
Organic pathology, 38
Ostfeld, 207
Oswald, 73, 208
Over-eating, 133–7

Paediatrics, 25, 199
Pain, 18, 19, 37–55, 166, 203
    behaviour, 54, 67
    cardiac, 50
    centres, 40
    chronic, 119, 122
    clinics, 53, 199
    complaints of, 38, 46, 49, 54, 67
    control, 68, 200
    dimensions of, 67
    experience, 38, 44, 47, 49, 54
    gate theory, 42
    intensity, 41, 49, 67
    killers, 41, 93
    locus of, 66
    personality differences, 48
    post-operative, 48, 168
    predictability, 48
    psychological factors, 38, 43–57, 68
    quality of, 66–7
    questionnaire, 67
    reaction component of, 50
    relief of, 51
    significance of, 42
    temporal, 50
    thresholds, 53, 55
    tolerance, 44–9
Parental visits, 174–5
Paresis, 152
Park, 209

Paskewitz, 210
Paternalistic medicine, 17
Patient-doctor relationship (*see* doctor-patient relationship)
Patients' satisfaction, 22, 26, 29
Patients' dissatisfactions, 22, 26, 29
Patterson, 18, 205
Paul, 99, 209
Peer models, 175–6
Penick, 137, 211
Personality disorder, 152
Persuasive communications, 33–6
Petrie, 49, 207
Phantom limb pain, 40
Phobias, 144–6
Pills, magic, 95–102
    sugar, 96–9, 128
Pilowsky, 47, 206
Placebo, 38, 64, 89–102, 195
Platt Committee, 169, 173
Prescriptions, 89, 90–3, 199
    behavioural, 196
Prevention of disease, 19
Professional disputes, 163
Prugh, 176, 213
Pseudo-patients, 91, 161–3
Psychoanalysis, 63, 98
Psychometric tests, 21, 139, 142
Psycholinguistics, 18
Psychological therapy, 141–8
Psychotherapy, 58, 63, 96, 141, 164
    non-directive, 143
Psychosis, 152

Rachman, 147, 205, 206, 207, 208, 209, 211, 212, 213
Raw, 131, 211
Recall, 29
Reduction, 49
Relaxation, 27, 55, 67, 81, 83, 114, 122
Relaxation training, 68

Index

Religious ceremonies, 38, 44
  healers, 158
REM (rapid eye movement),
  73–7, 86, 87
Retarded people, 178–92
Reward training, 18
Risley, 181, 213
Rogers, 143, 212
Rorschach test, 139–41, 162
Rosenhan, 91, 161–3, 209, 212
Royal College of Physicians,
  128
Royal College of Psychiatrists,
  160
Russell, 124, 125–6, 130, 211
Rutter, 172, 213

Sainsbury, 207
Sanity, 160–3
Schachter, 134–6, 211
Schizophrenia, 27, 141, 154,
  155, 181
Schumer, 211
Schwartz, B. A., 77, 208
Schwartz, G. E., 210
Selensky, 207
Self-control, 52, 68, 103–5,
  107, 108, 113–14, 128,
  130–1,133, 135–7
Self-help, 93, 202
Self-medication, 56, 93
Self-mutilation, 39, 53
Sexual disorders, 17, 147, 202
Sexual diversity, 150
Shapiro, A., 98, 209
Shapiro, D., 113, 210
Shepherd, 205, 208
Shneidman, 140, 211
Skinner, 147, 180–1, 213
Skin ointments, 93
Sleep, 70–88, 202
  amount of, 77
  deprivation, 74
  -lessness (see insomnia)
  needs, 79, 80

onset of, 79
psychological modification
  of, 80–4
rapid eye movements (see
  REM)
recovery, 74
satisfaction, 71, 76, 79, 82
Sleeping tablets (see hypnotics)
Slimming, 133
Smokers, 34, 123–33
Smoking, 33, 35, 123–33
Social Service Departments,
  21
Somnambulism, 70
Speech disorders, 17, 147
Spelman, 24, 27–8, 206
Spitz, 170
Spock, 18
Spontaneous improvements,
  143–4, 170
Sprague, 206
Stacey, 173–5, 213
Stanford University, 47
Steinmark, 81, 208
Stoyva, 114, 210
Stress, 165–8
Stuart, 136, 211
Stunkard, 134, 137, 211
Sugar pills, 96–9, 128
Suggestion, 43, 44, 52, 55
Surgery, 19, 41, 46, 51, 166–9,
  199
Surgical patients, 38, 166–9
Surgical ward, 23, 91

TAT, 139
Teasdale, 212
Temporalis muscle, 65
Tension, 114
Test-bashing, 139–41
Theodoridis, 213
Therapy, psychological, 141–8
Thomas, 211
Thompson, 178–9, 183, 213

222

Index

Toilet training, 85, 183–7, 189–90
Token economy, 20, 181–2
Tonsils, 169–70, 177
Toothache, 42
Torgenson, 67, 207
Tranquillisers, 64, 70, 96
Turner, 84, 99, 206, 208, 209
Tursky, 210

Uhlenhuth, 101, 210
Ulcers, 32, 122

Vasoconstriction, 60
Vasodilation, 60
Vasomotor, 60, 104, 108
VD sufferers, 36
Visual defects, 62
Visual prodromata, 59
Vitamins, 27, 90
Vomiting, 60
Von Frey, 40, 51

Wade, 91, 209
Wall, 37

Waters, 56, 59, 60, 62, 207
Weight reduction, 135, 136
Weiss, 116, 210
Wells, 210
Wenger, 107, 210
Werry, 209
Wetsz, 206
Wilkinson, 74, 79, 208
Williams, H., 33, 130, 206, 211
Williams, H. L., 74, 208
Wolf, 181, 213
Wolff, H. G., 206, 207
Wolpe, 144
Womb, 94
Wong, 213
Wood, 213
Woodrow, 206
Wounded soldiers, 41

Yale School of Nursing, 177
Yarrow, 172, 213
Yogi, 107
Young, 84, 99, 206, 208, 209

Zubin, 211